STEIN MART
AN AMERICAN STORY OF ROOTS, FAMILY, AND BUILDING A GREATER DREAM

STEIN MART
AN AMERICAN STORY OF ROOTS, FAMILY, AND BUILDING A GREATER DREAM

by

David J. Ginzl

With a Foreword by Eli N. Evans

University of Tampa Press
Tampa, Florida
2004

Manufactured in the United States of America
First Edition

The University of Tampa Press
401 West Kennedy Boulevard
Tampa, Florida 33606

ISBN: 1-879852-99-3

Library of Congress Cataloging-in-Publication Data

Ginzl, David J., 1947-
   Stein Mart : an American story of roots, family, and building a greater dream / by David J. Ginzl ; with a foreword by Eli N. Evans.-- 1st ed.
      p. cm.
   Includes bibliographical references.
   ISBN 1-879852-99-3 (cloth : alk. paper)
   1. Stein Mart--History. 2. Discount houses (Retail trade)--United States--History. 3. Stein, Jay, 1945- 4. Businesspeople--United States--Biography. I. Title.
   HF5465.U64S734 2004
   381'.141'092--dc22
                              2004004384

This book is dedicated

to all those who have made my life's work possible—

to my grandfather, whom I never knew, for taking the really big risk;

to my father and mother, who spent their lives making life better for me;

to my two daughters, Jay Meredith and Berry, who are the next generation

of this rich heritage and who make me so proud every single day; and

to my wife, Deanie, who has shared the growth of our company

and makes my life so worthwhile.

—Jay Stein

Contents

ILLUSTRATIONS

Jay Stein.

FOREWORD

A Tribute to Jay Stein: Boy Wonder

by Eli N. Evans

The story of Jews in the South, I often say, is the story of the fathers who built businesses for their sons who did not want them. But there is another paradigm, as well, rarely played out because it takes an extraordinary son to pull it off. It is the story of Leslie Wexner of The Limited in Columbus, Ohio; and Stanley Marcus of Neiman Marcus in Dallas, Texas; and yes, Jay Stein of Stein Mart in Greenville, Mississippi.

In a scene written by Mordecai Richler in his novel, *The Apprenticeship of Duddy Kravitz*, Duddy's uncle tells young Duddy the story of the "Boy Wonder," the legendary character of Jewish Montreal who arrived as a penniless immigrant and found a streetcar transfer on the street he promptly sold for three cents. According to the legend, that happenstance filled the boy's imagination with possibilities, and the "Boy Wonder" parlayed his pennies again and again until, ultimately, he returned to his old neighborhood in a white limousine.

Jay Stein is a Southern Jewish "Boy Wonder," who, as a boy in Greenville, Mississippi, working in his father's store — the very store his grandfather had started as an immigrant a generation before — spent summer afternoons watching the towboats and the barges on the river from the top of the giant levees and dreaming of a wider world. The Great River fired his imagination, and Jay Stein became a dreamer. And the dream never stopped. After college, he returned to Greenville for a few years to work in the original Stein Mart his father, Jake, had renamed in 1964 because a brother-in-law told him about a man named Sam Walton over in Arkansas and a discount idea named "Wal-Mart." So Jay's idea was inspired, not original, and he opened a second Stein Mart in Memphis, against his father's advice to just be happy with low-end merchandise in Greenville and who advised him, if he was bound and determined to go ahead, to set up a separate corporation so as "not to bring down the Greenville store." And just like the mythical "Boy Wonder," store by store, Jay built the Stein Mart idea into a nationwide chain of 260 stores across America with over 13,000 employees and, at its peak in 2000, $1.2 billion dollars in annual sales.

I first visited Greenville on a trip down the Mississippi River on a refurbished steamer called the *Delta Queen*. It didn't take too much effort to imagine the first Jews who came down this river like Jay's grandfather, Sam Stein, and walked off the boat at the Greenville dock, as we did. We looked over our shoulders as he must have done at the Big River, with currents bringing both opportunity and threat, with somewhat ominous giant levees to protect the town from the rising river, which, from time to time, became a torrent of angry water fierce enough to break through the levees and flood the town. The Hebrew Union Temple, built in 1906 to support the largest Jewish congregation in Mississippi, still stands. It is a magnificent domed structure, which began with a committed collection of ten men, rose in numbers, and then receded like the calmer tides of the summer, down to a much smaller congregation. To be there today is to be suspended in a dream, while time stands still; and there are moments to be savored, absorbed, and remembered, moments of time and the river.

The Jews like Sam Stein who came from Eastern Europe and Ellis Island to the Delta had helped to build Greenville and the surrounding towns, had been its peddlers and settlers, and then its merchants, its lawyers and doctors, its teachers, and in cities across the South, its mayors and aldermen. Of course, like Jews all across the small-town South, many of the children in the next generation left Greenville, but the Stein family stayed — at least Jay's parents, Jake and Freda, stayed — still running the store until Jake died and Jay's mother no longer was able to do it. Jay never forgot where he came from and who he was, no matter how successful he was. And when he looked for a larger progressive community in which to raise his daughters, an open community to live in and help lead, he selected Jacksonville, Florida, for the home office — site of a busy, growing, successful Jewish community and an inviting city with a civic spirit in an expanding region relatively near his Greenville origins.

The Stein Mart story suggests the continuation of something, not the end, the future linked to the past by common roots. Jay's new stores each followed the old traditions begun by his grandfather and his father. Stein Mart's corporate culture has been shaped and honed by those small-town years — the culture of community involvement, the culture of neighborliness. It is being a part of a place; not just another chain with indifferent owners, but a friendly place to serve the community and be welcoming and polite to the customers, and build a base, one customer at a time. Jay acknowledges that "my father left me his great name and reputation...[and] my mother gave me the compassion for others and I hope, her sweetness for her family and for all mankind." Even as Jay has become a major American philanthropist, and sits on the boards of the Kennedy Center in Washington, D.C., and New York University and was formerly vice chair of Hebrew Union College in New York, his story will always be attached to his origins, to his Jewish forbears. A major giver to the Holocaust Museum in Washington, D.C., he has not forgotten that his grandfather's shetl in Eastern Europe was destroyed by the Nazis. Jay's deep admiration for the early generations of immigrants in America and in Mississippi is a constant narrative of his inner voice. Their struggles will always be a part of him, as will the Great River that first brought his grandfather to the Delta, the mighty Mississippi flowing from its headwaters, like Southern Jewish history itself, alive and unfolding and flowing to the sea to what will be.

While this book is the story of a corporation, it is also the story of a family, and beyond that, it is really Jay's story. Jay has built the business store by store, taken the risks all along the way, and with each step, believed more and more in the future. Yet, in the book, out of an honest modesty (one of his best qualities), he was reticent to talk about his own role. He appropriately gives credit to his managers and executives like Jack Williams ("my right and left hands") and Carl Davis and Larry Shelton who ran the Memphis store, all of whom have been at his side for decades. Therefore, by his own preference, he is a somewhat opaque figure throughout the story you are about to read. Unspoken is a truth—he selected them, trusted them, rewarded them, and gave them the authority to succeed to the degree they refer to him and his parents "as much my family as my own." But Jay is the reason, the imagination, the entrepreneurial spirit, the visionary who has built Stein Mart.

Throughout his career, starting — like his father and grandfather before him — as a young man with a dream, he has been generous, restless, and bold. He is a man of genuine affection and affability (the book respects his privacy, but anyone who knows him can testify to his being a doting and involved father to his daughters). He is a common- sense person, and as an investor and builder of a nationwide business, he is a tremendously able man with remarkable intuition and an exquisite sense of timing. He has taste — as any retailer must have — and a life-long sense of good fashion. For example, walking with him down Fifth Avenue and looking at displays in store windows while listening to his running critique of the design and clutter and strategy, one gets a real education in the mercantile "show" that is implied in a window, how often it must change to show dynamism and seasonal sophistication, the place of wit and humor even, with subliminal messages to catch the imagination of a passerby.

To listen to Jay, one begins to sense that his stores are like "theaters," where the employees are "actors" in a play that Jay wants customers to remember and look forward to and revisit again and again. To get a sense of the corporate culture, just listen to the way a phone is answered all through the chain — "It's a great day at Stein Mart; how may I help you?" — or read the directions given to employees to "arrive at the store smiling," and at the end of the working day to "SMILE, you have had another great day." In the early years, he even could advise employees on how to dress and play their parts — for example to the "Boutique Ladies," one-day-a-week fashion-conscious women from the local com-munities (now numbering some 2,600 and once written up in the *Wall Street Journal*), who called their friends to report on bargains and gave fashion advice to other women and to men looking for gifts — the first handwritten rules in the Memphis store stated, "Please wear hose and do not chew gum." The Boutique Ladies received employee discounts as well, such that one husband complained, "You call this a job? I'm paying out more than she's ever going to bring in!" Jay is ever grateful for the community support, and after an opening sale, there usually is a large ad that exclaims, "Thank you, Little Rock [or whatever town].We love you too!" The style is exuberant, optimistic, welcoming. It's small town, too, no matter where a store is located.

Jay is constantly on the road visiting stores and opening new ones because he knows that his personal version of the Stein Mart tradition is harder and harder to infuse into the heart of his organization as the business gets larger and more far-flung. Yet he doesn't want the employees and the managers to miss knowing the history. He wants them to know of its roots, to believe in its personal style, to hear directly from him the keys to its success. He wants to tell the story and share its values. He visits the stock-rooms to shake hands with the burly crews who unload the merchandise, and greets the clerks and the maintenance men as well as the managers. Jay radiates confidence and warmth with his employees and works to continue to build "the family."

In fact, Jay's sense of an extended family and its history was the reason he asked David Ginzl to research, interview for, and write this book. Jay thought that a lot of employees deserved recognition for having spent their careers with the corporation, where he learned to recruit the best, train them in one store, and promote them to run a new one. And he felt that many long-time customers and friends, new and old, would be interested in the Stein Mart story and would share the book with their friends and family, as if they were sharing the story of themselves, because he deeply believes it is their story, too.

On January 6 of 2005, Jay will celebrate the100th anniversary of his grandfather Sam's arrival at Ellis Island with $43 in his pocket. I am sure Jay will recall how Sam became a delivery boy and saved the ten cents streetcar fare by walking all over New York City. He keeps in his offices in Jacksonville a renovated cash register from Greenville No. 1, displayed with the dignity of a sculpture, that serves as a reminder of his journey. I am sure that Jay's grandfather and father never even dreamed of a reality including hundreds of stores across America with the family name over them, but the small boy sitting on the levee of the Mississippi River did. Jay was then — and is still — the dreamer, the guiding force and big shoulders behind the story. He is the man who made it happen, the good son, and ultimately, looking back on all that has happened to him, the Southern Jewish "Boy Wonder," already a Mississippi legend.

Eli N. Evans is the author of *The Provincials: A Personal History of Jews in the South; Judah P. Benjamin: The Jewish Confederate;* and *The Lonely Days were Sundays: Reflections of a Jewish Southerner.*

INTRODUCTION

It is with mixed emotion on my part that this book is being written. Firstly, I am somewhat of a private person concerning my own personal life, and secondly, I question what interest it may have to the outside world.

Having said all that, I hope one day my children and then theirs and onward will reference this story to confirm the American Dream and to once again reflect on how it all happened. I suppose a very important part of the reason I am allowing the publication of this book is to acknowledge those folks who helped me make this dream possible.

I must always credit my forefathers and mothers for having taken the giant risk in coming to this strange land and planting that vital seed. I ask myself often, "Could I have done all that?" And my answer is still probably not. If my grandparents planted the seed, my parents nurtured it and made it blossom. My father really did develop the Stein Mart concept of value, built the foundation, and left me his great name and reputation in the community. My mother gave me the compassion for others and, I hope, her sweetness towards her family and all mankind.

Beyond my family's help comes everyone else—you can't write a history of Stein Mart without Jack Williams, who became both my right and left hands. Carl Davis, with the help of Larry Shelton, ran the great No. 2 store. If they hadn't done it so well, there wouldn't have been a No. 3, and so on. I can never say enough about those guys—they are and always will be "family."

The Company today is transformed from the small family business in which it began. It is clearly larger than I ever dreamed. I am confident that the team we have chosen will serve us well—and I look forward to many years of watching the abundant bounty being harvested from the seeds planted by my grandfather in the Mississippi Delta a century ago.

–Jay Stein
May 2003

Stein Mart

An American Story of Roots, Family, and Building a Greater Dream

1. Sam Stein.

CHAPTER 1

The Immigrant Peddler

"Few in number and unobtrusive in manner, most Southern Jews have seemed to want nothing more than to make a living... The peddlers were ubiquitous; Jews with an eye for the main chance founded stores like Garfinckel's in Washington, Thalhimer's in Richmond, Goldsmith's in Memphis, Neiman-Marcus in Dallas, Sakowitz's in Houston, Godchaux's in New Orleans, Cohen Brothers' in Jacksonville, Levy's in Savannah, and Rich's in Atlanta.... The traveler in the rural South can still observe how commonly the peddlers put down their packs to open stores and become pillars of the local community, can still lose count of the dry-goods stores, hardware stores, jewelry stores, clothing stores, and shoe stores that bear Jewish names."

> – Stephen J. Whitfield, "Jews and Other Southerners: Counterpoint and Paradox", in "*Turn to the South*": *Essays on Southern Jewry*

*T*he Stein Mart story begins in Greenville, Mississippi. It was there, just after the turn of the century, that Sam Stein, a young Jewish immigrant who spoke English with a thick accent, decided to make his new home. He soon found employment carrying a peddler's sack. With a variety of cheap household goods for sale, he visited the cabins and shacks of poor sharecroppers, both white and black. Traveling throughout the Mississippi Delta with a hundred-pound pack of merchandise on his back made for a hard, tiring life. But for Sam — and for many young Jews who drifted to the South – peddling marked the first step in building a better life. As difficult as peddling might be, Sam undoubtedly viewed his opportunities in Mississippi from the perspective of the conditions that he had left behind in eastern Europe.

Sam Stein was one among more than two million Jews who fled eastern Europe during the period from 1880 to 1920. Determined to escape the harsh, oppressive conditions that limited their economic prospects, they became part of a massive Jewish migration that included approximately one-third of all Jews who lived in the region. More than 80 percent of these Jewish immigrants chose to settle in the United States, which saw its Jewish population increase during these forty years from approximately 250,000 to 3.6 million.

As with so many of the immigrants from the late nineteenth and early twentieth centuries, details remain elusive about Sam Stein's youth and his migration to the United States. Sam left no written legacy. No letters or diaries recount his experiences. Neither he nor other family members of his generation wished to talk much about a past that held many unpleasant memories of hardships and disappointments, a past they would rather forget. On those few occasions when their thoughts did turn to "the old country" and to friends and relatives who had been left behind, they often would speak Yiddish so that the younger generations could not understand them. If pressed for information about their European roots, they would admonish their children and grandchildren not to look backward, but forward – "You are now an American." Nevertheless, from fragments of family history that have passed down to the present and from studying the larger immigration experiences of the millions who chose to leave eastern Europe, one can reconstruct a broad outline of Sam Stein's story.

The Stein family lived along the western fringe of the Russian Empire in the village of Amdur, located in the *gubernia*, or province, of Grodno. The Grodno area for centuries had found itself in the middle of the territorial ambitions of the Poles, the Lithuanians, and the Russians. It had been part of the Duchy of Lithuania, which in the mid-sixteenth century joined with the Kingdom of Poland in a loose, and at times uneasy, confederation under the rule of a common monarch. Between 1772 and 1795, its aggressively expansionist neighbors – Austria, Prussia, and Russia – dismembered the Polish-Lithuanian state in a series of partitions. Thus, the Grodno area came under Russian rule and remained so, except for a brief period in 1812-13 during Napoleon's invasion of Russia, until the First World War.

Sam Stein was born in 1882, the oldest of the fourteen children of Chaim and Chasha Stein. Whether the Steins should be considered Polish, Lithuanian, or Russian is open to question, dependent on the ever-changing borders. The key fact is that Sam had been born Jewish, which for him and other Jews represented the single overriding factor that defined their status and restricted their options. Life for Jews in eastern Europe, where approximately 75 percent of the world's nearly eight million Jews were then concentrated, could be harsh. For most of them, it meant poverty and constant hostility, interrupted by periodic outbreaks of violence.

In the last half of the nineteenth century, the peasant-based economy of czarist Russia underwent major disruptions caused by the modernization of agriculture, the emancipation of the serfs, and explosive population growth, leading to a long period of economic, political, and social instability. As often happens during times of turmoil, there was a search for scapegoats. Blame soon fell upon the Jews, whom the Russians had long regarded as "a pariah people." The czarist government issued draconian decrees – and urged strict enforcement of these discriminatory laws – forbidding Jews from owning land, limiting them to certain occupations, and forcibly relocating them into urban ghettos in the so-called "Pale of Settlement," twenty-five provinces in western Russia and Russian-controlled Poland. As one prominent leader of the Russian Orthodox Church explained, the official government policy hoped to eliminate all Jews: "one-third of the Jews will convert, one-third will die, and one-third will flee the country." Antisemitic propaganda received official sanction, and the government permitted – if not actually instigated – pogroms, mass violent attacks against Jewish communities, that periodically swept the area. Conditions worsened in the early 1900s as revolutionary movements opposed to the czarist government, many of which had very visible Jewish involvement, became more widespread, thus providing a pretext to unleash a series of especially violent pogroms from 1903 to 1906.[1]

The Grodno *gubernia* was one of the provinces within the Pale of Settlement. Twenty-five miles south of the city of Grodno, the administrative center for the province with that same name, was the *shtetl*, or village, of Amdur. At the end of the nineteenth century, Amdur had some 2,000 inhabitants, with 90 percent of them Jewish. Chaim Stein owned a bakery in Amdur. He was relatively well-to-do, with his bakery on the ground floor of a brick building and the family living quarters above the shop. One of his daughters later recalled that the brick home had wooden floors, in contrast to the wooden homes and dirt floors of many of their neighbors. Chaim's prominent status in the community is illustrated further by his inclusion on the voting lists for the 1912 elections to the Russian parliament, or *Duma*. Generally, Jews were not permitted to vote, as they were considered non-Russians. The fact that Chaim, as well as his brother Kasrel, made the voter roll indicates that he had achieved a certain elevated status.

Not only was the Stein family prosperous, but the village of Amdur seemed to have been spared much of the hostility and violence prevalent elsewhere in the Pale. In the early 1900s, several pogroms broke out just south of Amdur in Bialystok, a major textile manufacturing center in which Jews constituted a majority of the population. But no pogroms terrorized Amdur, and this avoidance of officially sanctioned antisemitic actions may explain Chaim Stein's continued loyalty toward the czarist government. Nevertheless, the fear of arbitrary violence from the gentiles, or *goyim*, and especially from roving bands of armed, undisciplined Cossacks, remained always present.

Actually, Chaim Stein and his family may have had more to fear from fellow Jews than from the gentiles. Chaim's youngest daughter, Tillie, in a videotaped interview when in her eighties, remembered that some Jewish revolutionaries opposed to the czarist regime tried to blow up the Stein's bakery and home. They targeted Chaim because he held a government position as a *starosta*, or magistrate. Chaim was very proud of his official status and always voiced support for the czar. On Fridays, Chaim's bakery would prepare its ovens so as to keep the family's food warm during the *Shabbat*, or Sabbath, when observant Jews could do no work. He also would place in the ovens pots of stew brought by neighbors. One Sabbath eve, after Sam had already left for America, a heavy, unusual-looking pot was left at the bakery. One of Chaim's daughters, Leah, opened the pot and seeing a layer of dry potatoes covering the top, added water before placing it in the oven. When no one claimed the pot after the Sabbath, Chaim opened it and found, beneath the potatoes, a bomb. Fortunately for the family, the added water had kept it from detonating when placed in the oven.

Observance of the religious and dietary laws dominated daily life for the Jews in the Amdur *shtetl*. For centuries Amdur had had a largely Jewish population and had been a noteworthy religious center that

2. A formal family portrait of the Steins in 1911. In the back row, from the left, are Bashi, Leah, and Tevel; in the middle row, Chasha, Chaim, and Baruch; in the front is Tillie. Yakov was also present in the photography studio, but he refused to be in the picture because he feared the powder flash used by the photographer.

produced prominent rabbis and religious scholars. It also had a number of adherents of Hasidism, a movement that advocated more spirituality in religious life and promoted the Jewish settlement of Palestine. There were several synagogues in the village, with the most dominant being a large brick synagogue, or great *shul*, built in 1882 – the same year that Sam Stein was born – after a fire had destroyed most of the town. This synagogue is still standing more than a century later, although the village is now called Indura and is located in Belarus, which since the 1991 break-up of the Soviet Union has been an independent state. But there are no Jews in Indura, all of them having been sent to Nazi concentration camps during World War II. Either none survived the Holocaust, or the few who did chose not to return to their homes. The brick synagogue, in disrepair, is now used as a warehouse.

Little is known about Sam Stein's youth in Amdur. Sam, which is the anglicized form of his Yiddish name, Shmuel, certainly worked in the family bakery and, as the oldest child, was being groomed by his father to take over the business. Life in the Stein household would have been crowded. In addition to his brothers and sisters, his grandfather, Baruch Stein, lived into his nineties and stayed with the family. His Uncle Kasrel, Chaim's brother, owned another bakery in Amdur. Kasrel Stein and his wife Freda had several children, one of whom, Eugene, later settled in Chicago, where he too owned a bakery. There undoubtedly were other members of the extended family, but the memories of those aunts and uncles and cousins have been lost.

Of Sam's thirteen siblings, only seven lived to adulthood. And four of them eventually immigrated to the United States. After Sam led the way, his brother Yakov, or Jacob (or simply Jake), followed, settling in Mount Pleasant, Tennessee, where he opened a general merchandise store. Tevel, or Tobias, immigrated first to Portugal, where his wife had a brother, and then to the U.S. during World War II. Of Sam's five sisters – Sarah, Leah, Jennie, Bashi, and Tillie – Jennie came to Arcola, Mississippi, where she married Jacob Frank, who also operated a general merchandise store. Jennie raised money – and one suspects that her brothers Sam and Jake contributed to the effort – to bring her sister Leah to America. But Leah died during the worldwide influenza epidemic that followed the end of World War I, so the youngest sister, Tillie, took her place, arriving in the U.S. in 1921. Tillie went to Arcola, and then to Greenville to meet her brother Sam, who had left Amdur before she had been born. Tillie soon moved to Mount Pleasant and worked in her brother Jake's store, eventually marrying her sister-in-law's brother, Abe Rosenberg, who also operated a dry goods store in the town.

As for Sam Stein, he emerged from obscurity in early 1904 at the outset of the Russo-Japanese War. The twenty-two-year-old Stein had been drafted into the Russian Army. His prospects appeared bleak, as Jewish conscripts faced twenty-five-year enlistments. This lengthy military obligation had little practical importance since the likelihood of Sam surviving that long appeared doubtful. With war imminent, Jews and others deemed to be undesirables most likely would be placed on the front lines as cannon fodder. After completing his military training, but prior to being shipped to the front, Sam requested a furlough, which a sympathetic Russian officer granted. Back at home, Sam had no intention of returning to the military, instead determining that he wished to go to America. He asked his father for help, but the elder Stein refused. Years earlier, Chaim had traveled to the United States, but soon returned when he found that Jews in America did not regularly observe the Sabbath or follow other religious laws. He considered America to be a godless place and forbade any of his children from going there. Sam needed his father's help, since as a municipal official Chaim had the notary-type seal necessary to authenticate travel documents. Not to be deterred, Sam enlisted his mother's help, broke into his father's desk, stole travel documents and some money, and fled westward toward Germany. The next day, upon discovering the theft, Chaim reported his son to the Russian authorities, but by then Sam had gone far enough to elude any pursuers.

From Amdur, Sam made his way to the German port of Hamburg, on the Baltic Sea. Details of his journey are unknown. Whether he traveled by foot, or by wagon, or if he had taken sufficient funds to afford a railway ticket, it must have been an arduous trip. Crossing the Russian-German border would have been a dangerous undertaking as he, a military deserter, carried stolen and forged travel documents. Even after making it safely into Germany, Sam surely led a precarious existence as he sought shelter and food along the way, while trying to preserve as much money as possible in order to purchase a ticket on a trans-Atlantic ship, as well as the food and supplies necessary for the two-week passage. He eventually purchased a ticket on the *Grafwaldersee*, a 2,546-passenger ship on the Hamburg-American line. The *Grafwaldersee* departed from Hamburg on December 23, 1904. Crossing the North Atlantic in late December and early January had to be cold and unpleasant, especially since Sam found himself with 2,200 other third-class passengers crammed into overcrowded and often unsanitary conditions below deck in steerage, the cheapest accommodations available. The *Grafwaldersee* arrived at Ellis Island, New York City, on January 5, 1905.

According to the ship's manifest, Sam Stein arrived in New York with $43 in his possession, which represented approximately four or five weeks of wages for an unskilled worker. He told immigration officials that he planned to stay with a cousin named Lieb Meadow, who lived in New York City. This cousin was in the coat manufacturing business, and for several months Sam worked for him as a messenger and courier. Sam liked neither his job nor New York City. As his son Jake later recalled, "He was paid a very meager sum of money in salary. He often told me that his savings were not from his salary because it took all the money he made to live on. His savings came when he was given a package or letter or anything to carry, he was also given the dime to ride the subway. He would walk and put the dime in his pocket and save it. That was his savings." And when he had saved enough money to leave New York, Sam headed west to Memphis, Tennessee.

Why Sam Stein headed to Memphis is unclear. Most Jews, whether because of inertia or fear, did not venture far from New York City, where they often found some sense of security in the familiar foods, cultures, and languages of the crowded Jewish ghettos that had developed in the city. Those who left generally did so only if a friend or relative had already gone before them and promised to help them get established. But Sam had no such friend or relative in the West or South, only an adventurous spirit and a willingness to work hard. After arriving in Memphis, Sam became a peddler of costume jewelry, carrying a pack of glittering trinkets on a regular route through the city and surrounding rural areas. Again, he soon looked for better opportunities. He took a packet boat down the Mississippi River, visiting various river towns to assess business prospects. When Sam reached Greenville, Mississippi, in late 1905 or early 1906, he decided to stay.

The decision to settle in Greenville is easy to understand. The city was a vibrant commercial center for the Mississippi Delta and the large cotton-growing farms that dominated the local economy. For a Southern town, Greenville had a surprisingly diverse population, with large numbers of Italians, Chinese, and Jews. The substantial Jewish presence would have been readily apparent to young Sam Stein as he wandered the principal business district along Washington Avenue, where many stores and shops were owned and operated by men with names like Blum, Brill, Cohn, Goldman, and Weinberg. One block south on Main Street, construction had begun on a massive stone building with Greek columns that would be the new Hebrew Union Temple. When completed in 1906, the synagogue would be the spiritual center for the largest Jewish congregation in the state of Mississippi. Greenville certainly appeared to be a town where an ambitious young Jew could feel comfortable, put down roots, and prosper.

Within a short time, Sam undoubtedly learned about the extent of Jewish involvement in Greenville's civic and business circles. The town had been destroyed by Union troops during the Civil War, and in 1865 the "new" Greenville emerged one mile north of the original location. Morris Weiss opened the first store there, and other Jewish merchants soon followed. The state legislature approved the formal incorporation of the town in 1870, by which time enough Jewish families had moved to the area to organize a congregation. In 1879, they reorganized as the Hebrew Union Congregation and the following year built the town's first synagogue. Meanwhile, the growing Jewish community played an influential role in city government, with Jacob Alexander and Leopold Wilczinski among its first mayors and a number of other Jewish citizens serving on the city council, various municipal boards, and committees.[2]

Little overt antisemitism surfaced and the Greenville community remained open to full Jewish participation. Only in death were Jews segregated, buried in a separate cemetery according to Jewish law and tradition following the devastating 1878 yellow fever epidemic that killed nearly one-third of the town's residents. With this one exception – a segregation of the dead into four separate cemeteries reserved for white Christians (both Protestants and Catholics), Jews, Chinese, or African-Americans – Jews found themselves fully accepted into Greenville's business, political, civic, and social activities, and over the years Greenville gained a reputation as the most tolerant and enlightened city in Mississippi.

Thus did Sam Stein decide to make Greenville his home. He began peddling jewelry, and later other merchandise as well, along a route between Greenville and Vicksburg. At first, he traveled on foot, and later purchased a horse and buggy. For the handful of Jews who ventured into the South, peddling cheap clothes, buttons, needles, and various household items to both blacks and poor whites often represented the first step in establishing a mercantile business. As one historian has observed, "Many a Southern store had its beginnings in a humble peddler's pack."[3]

Peddling is perhaps best described by David Cohn, one of a number of prominent writers from Greenville. Cohn's father had established one of Greenville's earliest Jewish-owned stores, The Fair, and he himself had been a retailer (including, briefly, national sales manager for Sears Roebuck) before turning to writing. In Cohn's memoirs, published posthumously, he described a peddler as "a walking store." Cohn explains, "Lowliest of businessmen, his were the lowliest of customers: Negroes and poor whites who lived in cabins encompassed by forests slowly yielding to fire and ax." To succeed, peddling "demanded stoic endurance of its practitioners, the capacity to suffer cruel hardships, and the willingness to suffer them for small money rewards." To get started, a peddler required only a minimal capital investment, along with a strong back to carry a pack that often weighed more than one hundred pounds and the courage to venture forth into a rough and potentially violent countryside. As Cohn points out, "No large experience was required and a man could learn as he earned. Peddling, moreover, enabled a man to earn a living in a severe school while perfecting his knowledge of the language and customs of the country."[4]

As the peddler traveled through countryside Cohn described as "largely crude" where "roads were mule-belly deep in mud during winter and stifling with dust in summer," he faced harsh weather, swarms of mosquitoes, uncertain accommodations, and sometimes violence.[5] While traveling his route to Vicksburg, two men jumped Sam outside the town of Redwood, shot him in the arm, and stole his merchandise. His wounds must have been serious, as he spent several months in a Vicksburg hospital before returning to Greenville. He never fully recovered strength in his right arm. Back in Greenville, Sam began selling merchandise out of a suitcase on the streets, finding an especially lucrative spot near the corner of Washington and Walnut Streets in front of Finlay's Drug Store. A friend named J. Romanski suggested that Sam open a permanent store rather than sell off the street. Romanski worked as a jobber, a middleman who purchased merchandise from manufacturers and then sold it to retail merchants. He offered to finance Sam's stock of merchandise. Sam Stein then leased his first storefront, only twenty by twenty-five feet, on Walnut Street. The exact date remains shrouded in uncertainty, but it was probably sometime in 1908 when this first Stein store opened.

Several years after opening his Walnut Street store, Sam married Fannie Aarenzon. She too was a Russian immigrant, from the city of Brest-Litovsk (which a decade later would gain notoriety as the site where Germany and Russia signed a separate peace treaty ending their World War I conflict). Her family had been terrorized by the pogroms, and her mother had a saber scar across her face as a reminder of the violence and hatred that they had left behind. Fannie's father, Aaron Aarenzon, had come to America first, settling in Greenwood, Mississippi, where he opened a shoe store. He sent for his wife and six daughters later as he saved enough money to finance their passages.

3. & 4. Sam Stein and Fannie Aarenzon Stein.

Fannie and one of her sisters made the journey in 1909. Speaking no English, they traveled with notes clipped to the front of their clothing, with instructions that they be delivered to their relatives in Greenwood. Given that Greenwood is located fifty miles east of Greenville, how Sam Stein and Fannie Aarenzon met is unclear, although one suspects that some matchmaking efforts from the Jewish communities in both towns played a role in the courtship. Fannie was not yet twenty, and nearly a decade younger than Sam. Nevertheless, within months of her arrival, Fannie and Sam married.

Sam and Fannie soon started a family. Fannie returned to her parents in Greenwood for the birth of their first child, Jake, a son born on March 16, 1911, and named after one of Sam's brothers, Yakov. It is not clear whether he was actually named Jacob (as listed on the 1920 census report) or simply Jake. In any case, no one ever called him anything other than Jake. Three other Stein children followed – Joseph (born September 8, 1912), Sadie Lee (born August 18, 1914), and Bernard (born January 9, 1919).

While details about the management and sales volume of the small store on Walnut Street, located just across from the levee that held back the Mississippi River, do not exist, Sam Stein's business evidently prospered. He made several small expansions to the store, and began

5. *Jennie Stein Frank and her son Mose in the general store owned by Jennie's husband, Jacob Frank, in Arcola, Mississippi. There are no surviving photographs of the inside of Sam Stein's store, but it undoubtedly looked similar to this store.*

specializing in clothing, shoes, fabrics, and household goods for work-ing-class families. The business provided sufficient money to support his growing family and, after the birth of his second son, to hire a domestic servant – a young black woman named Miss Ollie Bell – to help with the cleaning, cooking, and the raising of the children. He purchased a house at 403 Central Avenue, several blocks from his store, and accord-ing to information provided to the 1920 census-taker, he owned his home with no mortgage encumbering the property.

While other Jewish-owned merchandise stores such as The Fair and Nelms and Blum appealed to a more upscale clientele, as did specialty shops like Johl & Bergman shoes and Dave Weinberg's ladies' shop, Sam focused on the same type of customers with whom he had become familiar during his time as a peddler. His store, called simply Sam Stein, stocked lower-price merchandise that was affordable to workers in town and to tenants and sharecroppers who worked the large farms surrounding Greenville. His customers included both blacks and less affluent whites.

During these early years, the small store on Walnut Street undoubtedly faced some challenging times. Shortly after arriving in Greenville, Sam would have learned how closely the prosperity of both the town and surrounding Washington County was tied to "King Cotton," the cash crop grown throughout the rich agricultural lands of the Mississippi Delta stretching for nearly 150 miles from just south of Memphis to Vicksburg. In the vivid prose of David Cohn: "Cotton is more than a crop in the Delta. It is a form of mysticism. It is a religion and a way of life. Cotton is omnipresent here as god is omnipresent.... In an age of machines, the patient mule lost in prehistoric thought, followed by a plodding Negro down a turnrow, remains the machine age of the Delta."[6]

The importance of cotton to the local Greenville economy was evident from the bustling activity at the commercial trading houses that lined "Cotton Row" along Main Street, only several blocks from the Stein store. Since Sam had settled in Greenville, times had been good, with increased levels of cotton production each year and rising cotton prices. The outbreak of World War I in August 1914, however, caused disruptions in the export of cotton overseas and led to economic hardships throughout the Delta. The price of cotton plummeted, with the value of that year's crop, soon to be picked, slashed by approximately one-half. Cotton prices remained depressed for the next several years. For Sam Stein and other storeowners, these years must have been difficult ones with the local economy so dependent on cotton. The economic downturn impacted both sales and the collection of accounts in those cases where credit had been extended. Business conditions did not improve until after the United States entered the war in early 1917.

Although Sam and Fannie both had become naturalized U.S. citizens in 1912, the outbreak of the war found Sam in his late thirties, with a family to support, so he did not get called to military service. The war, however, returned prosperity to the Delta, if only for a brief period. Cotton prices soared to record highs, bringing increased profits to the cotton growers and traders and putting more money into the hands of working people who could then purchase better clothes and more household goods. Businesses flourished. But these same high prices soon led to disaster, as they encouraged the growers to seek ever greater cotton production, which then resulted, in the summer of 1920, in what has been described as "the most dramatic collapse in cotton history."[7] Cotton prices that had risen to 40 cents per pound spiraled downward, and by year-end cotton was selling for only 13.5 cents per pound.

This post-war agricultural slump had significant repercussions for Sam Stein, who now faced a severe "financial crisis." In the spring of 1920, when business conditions had been booming, Sam traveled to St. Louis where he purchased a large stock of merchandise. As his son Jake later recalled, "those goods were not worth thirty cents on the dollar when it was time to sell them in October." Sam avoided disaster only because his banker agreed to work with him through this difficult time, obviously a reflection of the excellent business reputation that he had built during the prior decade. According to Jake's recollection, a number of businesses "went broke," but Sam managed to survive – "Thanks to the Citizens Bank of Greenville and its chief operating officer, Frank Robertshaw… my father did not have to go bankrupt. Mr. Robertshaw told him to make out checks to everybody he owed. The bank would pay the checks and he could pay the bank when he could. So my father stayed open and paid off and the Stein business continued through that crisis."

The recession of 1920 struck not only cotton, but it impacted nearly all agricultural commodities throughout the country. It represented the beginning of two decades of economic hardships and struggles through-out rural America, years that would be especially difficult for Mississippi and for a cotton industry in severe decline because of overproduction, falling prices, and the spreading boll-weavil infestation. Despite this bleak economic climate, Sam Stein found a way to repay his debts, rebuild his finances, and expand his business. Four years later, in 1924, he had sufficient funds to purchase a vacant store at 207 Washington Avenue and move his business there. With a larger store, Fannie and the older children started working more at the business. Jake began working afternoons after school and weekends at the age of twelve, and his brother Joe soon joined him. The Stein family would operate a retail store on the 200 block of Washington Avenue for the next seventy-two years.

Several years after moving to Washington Avenue, Sam Stein faced perhaps his biggest challenge – the Mississippi River flood of 1927. The Delta region periodically had suffered from devastating floods as the Mississippi overflowed its banks and its waters spread across the broad expanses of flat agricultural lands. Townspeople still talked about the legendary flood of 1882, and in subsequent years the Mississippi River

6. *Downtown Greenville had flooding problems for months following the April 1927 levee break. This photo, taken from the levee where thousands of displaced black laborers lived in tents and other temporary shelters, shows the main business district along Washington Avenue. Sam Stein's store at 207 Washington Avenue is indicated by the arrow.*

7. The Fair, located in the 400 block of Washington Avenue during the 1927 flood, was one of Greenville's oldest retail stores, established in 1896 by Jules Whitney and Henry Cohn. Shortly after its opening, Cohn's cousin, Ben Nelkin, became a partner and later sole owner, and The Fair remained in the Nelkin family for three generations before finally closing in 1986. The Fair moved from its 401 Washington Avenue location in 1931. Sam Stein's relocated to this building in 1950.

actually had shifted, forming a new channel and causing several blocks of downtown Greenville buildings to collapse into the river. In response, a new earthen levee had been constructed, with concrete then poured over it to reinforce its strength, thus creating a huge, sloping wharf hundreds of yards in length. This new levee had succeeded in preventing any catastrophes, although there still had been some periodic flooding problems. But 1927 would be different, and when a levee north of the city broke in late April, panic engulfed Greenville and the entire Delta. William Alexander Percy, member of one of the Delta's most prominent planter families and the person who coordinated the Red Cross relief efforts in Greenville that year, described the 1927 flood as "a torrent ten feet deep the size of Rhode Island; it was thirty-six hours coming and four months going; it was deep enough to drown a man, swift enough to upset a boat, and lasting enough to cancel a crop year."[8] The raging floodwaters completely washed away more than 2,200 buildings in the Delta, damaged thousands more, and according to the Red Cross killed 120 people, an official estimate considered too small by at least half. A recent historical study of the flood reported, "Of all the counties in the entire flooded region, from Illinois to the Gulf of Mexico, Washington County [Greenville] was the single one that suffered the most devastating losses."[9] And the waters did not fully recede until mid-August.

In the weeks prior to the levee break on April 21, reports of flooding along the upper Mississippi River prompted Greenville's citizens to prepare for the worst. At the Stein store, Sam and his two oldest sons, Jake and Joe, "stood there day and night trying to raise everything we could up to the five-foot level." After doing all that was possible to protect the store and his stock of merchandise, Sam sent Fannie and the three younger children on one of the last trains out of Greenville. They stayed with Fannie's family in Greenwood, a town that also faced flooding problems but not nearly the potential devastation to be found in Greenville. Sam and Jake stayed behind to watch over the store as best they could.

Jake later described the 1927 flood as a "setback to the business," a huge understatement given the lost sales and damage to merchandise and the store. Remarkably the Sam Stein store reopened, on a limited basis, within two weeks. After the floodwaters struck the city, Sam helped deliver the mail that arrived by steamboats from Memphis and Vicksburg. Jake worked at a soup kitchen set up to feed the nearly 13,000 black refugees who had fled to town from surrounding rural areas, and who now found themselves confined to the top of the narrow levee with little shelter and no supplies. In their free time, both Sam and his son worked to get the store ready for business. Scaffolding had been erected and boardwalks built from the levee down the city's two principal streets, Washington Avenue and Main Street. After the boardwalk reached the Sam Stein store at 207 Washington Avenue, Sam posted a notice in the May 3 edition of Greenville's *Daily Democrat-Times*, which continued publishing throughout the flooding even though reduced to a single front-and-back sheet. The advertisement read, "Sidewalks Into Our Store. The floors are dry and we have a complete stock at less than pre-flood prices."

One questions how ready for business the Sam Stein store really was. In early May, the river continued above flood stage, water still flowed through the levee breaks, and downtown Greenville remained flooded. The cleaning of the downtown would take months, with mud from the rich Delta soil caked everywhere, not to mention buildings infested with snakes and frogs and the stench of dead fish. One prominent Greenville attorney warned his family not to venture downtown: "Every store in town, when opened to be cleaned, smells horribly, and the entrance to the Weinberg Building is like walking into a sewer. . . . Newspapers are very misleading in their reports of openings."[10] Nevertheless, Sam Stein reopened, as did all other retail stores as the boardwalk reached their doors, if only for a few hours each day. Slowly, business returned to some semblance of normality during the summer of 1927.

Over the next several years, Sam focused on rebuilding his home and his business. A fire had damaged the Stein home at the corner of Central Avenue and Shelby Street several months before the 1927 flood and the family had been forced to live in rented rooms until evacuating to Greenwood. Soon after the floodwaters receded, Sam acquired a large home in a more upscale neighborhood at 1212 Washington Avenue. In 1928, he moved his business to a still larger location on Washington Avenue, one that had previously been occupied by the Geise-Mann Hardware Store. As Jake recalled, "This was a very nice store in the same block. It gave us the opportunity to handle more merchandise and to cater to a larger population. Greenville was growing fast and Sam Stein was keeping pace."

Despite the business difficulties created by the 1927 flood and the spreading economic problems caused by the 1929 stock market crash and the onset of the Great Depression, Sam Stein had the financial resources in 1930 to travel to Europe to visit his widowed mother. Two years earlier, his sister Tillie, married and living in Mount Pleasant, Tennessee, had made this same visit, and her mother had confided that her one wish before she died was to see her oldest son again. At that time, Chasha Stein lived in Bialystok, where she had moved after the death of her husband to live with the family of her daughter Bashi. Bialystok had been in the Grodno province, which during World War I had been occupied by the German Army, and after the war fought over by the Russians and Poles. The Treaty of Riga in 1921 made the Grodno province part of the new Poland that had been created in the aftermath of the war. Thus, in the summer of 1930, Sam headed to Poland, booking passage on the White Star Line and traveling in far more comfortable accommodations than he had twenty-five years earlier. His brother Tobias, who then lived in Portugal, met him and together they traveled to Bialystok. Sam spent nearly two months in Europe, visiting his mother but also traveling in Belgium, the Netherlands, and Germany before returning home.

Through hard work and determination, Sam Stein had created a good life for himself and his family in Greenville. He was successful and well-respected in the community. Then suddenly, at the relatively young age of fifty, he dropped dead. Each day, Sam would leave his store and go to a nearby pool hall, the Smoke House, for lunch. On February 22, 1933, having finished his meal and purchased an after-lunch cigar, Sam suffered a massive heart attack. The report of his death in the *Daily Democrat-Times* described how "a pall of sorrow has been cast over the city" by the sudden death of "one of Greenville's most successful merchants." The next day, the newspaper carried an editorial, entitled "A Man of Courage," expressing the "universal sorrow" at his death, which represented "a distinct loss to the community." Commenting on his "characteristic smile" and his " undefeatable spirit," the editorial noted how much Sam Stein had accomplished since arriving in Greenville with few earthly possessions a quarter of a century earlier. It concluded, "His was a hard fight – one that would have discouraged most of us and one that would have been met with defeat by many of us. We need more men like him."

8. *Jake Stein.*

CHAPTER 2

The Delta Merchant

"I soon noticed that in Mississippi one spoke not of going to Clarksdale, Greenville, or Greenwood, but of traveling 'into the Delta,' the implication being that of passage back in time, to a setting that—if such a thing were possible—seemed even more southern than the rest of the state…. [A]s my research progressed I grew to regret my impressionistic observations, not because I had exaggerated the Delta's southerness, but because I had oversimplified and, to some extent, trivialized it. The Delta that ultimately emerged from my study was no mere isolated backwater where time stood still while southerners stood fast. Indeed, many of the major economic, political, and social forces that have swept across the American landscape during the last 150 years have actually converged in the Mississippi Delta."

– James C. Cobb, *The Most Southern Place on Earth: The Mississippi Delta and the Roots of Regional Identity.*

Sam Stein's death had come at an unfortunate time, as February 1933 found Mississippi on the verge of economic collapse. The state's agriculture-based economy had never fully recovered from the post-World War I recession. Farm incomes plummeted during the 1920s as the price of cotton, the principal cash crop, fell to only 4.6 cents per pound, the lowest price since the depression of the mid-1890s. The financial difficulties facing farm families rippled through the state's economy.[1] By January 1933, the director of the State Board of Public Welfare reported that more than 600,000 people, nearly one-third of the state's population, received funds from the state board, either through "work relief" projects or "direct relief" payments to destitute families.

This increased demand for relief services stretched the financial resources of Mississippi's state and local governments. The state debt increased dramatically while tax revenues declined, thus raising concerns about the state's creditworthiness. Local governments faced insolvency, with insufficient funds to pay teachers, many whom did not receive their salaries but instead certificates of indebtedness, with the amount on the certificates subject to significant discounting when cashed. Foreclosure sales for failure to pay property taxes accelerated and left thousands homeless. The state's banking commissioner issued a directive limiting the amounts that depositors could withdraw from their banking accounts, thus adding Mississippi to a lengthening list of states that had declared so-called "bank holidays."

It was in the midst of this economic crisis that Sam Stein died, at the bleakest point of the Great Depression. With business failures increasing and unemployment soaring, a general sense of foreboding had settled over the entire country. By this last week in February, a nervous populace awaited the inauguration, still nearly two weeks away, of the newly elected Franklin D. Roosevelt and worried whether or not the new president could reverse the nation's economic troubles. The Stein family faced the additional worry of whether or not the family business could survive.

Sam's widow, Fannie, had worked intermittently in the store for more than twenty years, but her role had been restricted to waiting on customers and collecting their cash. She had no managerial experience and knew nothing about purchasing merchandise. Sam had begun training his two oldest sons to manage the store, but his premature death left them feeling unprepared for the challenges they would face. As Jake recalled years later, "His death left the store to Joe and myself. I did not know what to do. I had worked at the store after school days in high school. I knew something about running the store, but about managing it, dealing with the public, I knew very little, and I was still only twenty-one."

Jake Stein may have been young and inexperienced, but he had the advantage of being well-known in the Greenville community. As in most Southern towns, Greenville was obsessed with football and, in this pre-television era, with its local high school team. Jake loved football. Even though both his parents were short but heavyset, Jake grew to be six feet tall and weighed over 200 pounds, a dominating physical presence for his day. In the fall of 1928, the Greenville High School "Hornets" went undefeated, with only a tie against rival Greenwood marring their record. But several schools complained that Greenville High had an assistant coach who was not employed by the school system and thus, according to the high school yearbook, "objections were raised by neighboring school authorities and the 'Hornets' right for consideration in the Delta championship attacked. The objections were sustained by both the Delta and State Associations and the crown was handed to Greenwood, a team whose record for the season was far from equalling that of the Hornets." Jake and Joe Stein—both members of the junior class, even though Jake was a year and a half older—played on the team, which the local newspaper subsequently referred to as the "Uncrowned Champs." But Jake was the star and elected captain of the team for his senior year. The next year, with Jake at tackle and Joe playing quarterback, Greenville High had high hopes for winning the championship that had been taken away the year before, but two losses eliminated them from consideration. Nevertheless, during Greenville's victory over rival Greenwood, the local newspaper reported, "Captain Jake Stein, who played in his 24th consecutive game without being substituted, certainly proved how he accomplished this record. The weighty tackle now holds the high school record for the number of games played in." After being the biggest star on his high school team, Jake went to the University of Alabama in the fall of 1930 with hopes of playing college football. That year, the Crimson Tide went undefeated and won the Rose Bowl on New Year's Day, 1931. Unfortunately, Jake's football career at Alabama was hampered by injuries and he never earned his varsity letter. He left college after one year and returned to Greenville to work in the family business, thus allowing his brother Joe to attend the University of Alabama for a year. Even though he never achieved success at the college level, Jake benefitted from his football exploits—or perhaps, more accurately, from the memories of those football days, for the stories only became more impressive in the retelling and served him well in the years ahead.

Not only was Jake—and to a lesser extent, Joe—well-known and well-liked, but both young men had a reservoir of good will to draw on. Sam Stein had lived in Greenville for more than twenty-five years, and the Stein family had established strong roots in the community. Sam had been popular in the town and at the Hebrew Union Temple. The Jewish merchants and others in the Jewish community now stood ready to offer advice and assistance to the family. Jake also sought the counsel of the store's suppliers: "To make the decision on whether to keep the store, I went to St. Louis to take this matter up with one of our chief creditors and suppliers. He said 'I want you to go back and take care of your mother and three kids. Forget what you owe us. You pay us whenever you can. You call me every ten days and tell me what you did the past ten days and I'll tell you what to do the next ten days.' This went on for approximately a year." Just as a cooperative local banker had stood by Sam Stein during his financial problems in 1920, now one of the store's principal suppliers, who had built a strong rapport with Sam over the years, offered that same level of support to his sons.

Only a week after Sam's death, the Steins purchased a full-page advertisement in the *Daily Democrat-Times* to announce a "Sam Stein's Administrator's Sale," beginning March 2, "on account of the sad loss of our leader Mr. Sam Stein." This ad, together with a series of advertisements in the weeks to come, represented a sharp departure from past practices. Sam Stein had, on occasion, placed notices in the local newspaper, but seldom advertised merchandise. Breaking with past practices, this ad listed dozens of bargains, ranging from "full cut" men's overalls at 47 cents to silk dresses for $1.58 to an assortment of fabrics at 5 cents per yard. "The people of this community have always enjoyed the privilege of saving on every purchase," the advertisement promised, "and now we offer you at sale prices the biggest values ever presented in our history."

The sale proved a huge success, necessitating a follow-up "Thank You Greenville" announcement in the newspaper expressing appreciation to "the crowd that thronged our store," even though "personal attention could not be given everyone." The announcement also mentioned new merchandise that kept arriving and that was being placed on the tables as "Saturday's Special." The successful sales during these first weeks of March 1933—despite the bleak economic conditions—convinced Jake and Joe (and one suspects their mother, Fannie) that they could manage the Sam Stein store and make a profit doing so. Consequently, on March 21, Jake and Joe again used the local newspaper to disclose their decision "as to whether we intend to carry on the business of our father." The announcement stated, "We wish to take this opportunity to advise you that this business WILL BE CARRIED ON by us on exactly the same principles as before, and we will continue to offer to the people of Greenville and surrounding territory the same high grade

9. *An advertisement in the* Daily Democrat-Times *announced a March 2 "Administrator's Sale" following Sam Stein's death.*

merchandise at popular prices as in previous years." The ad then pointed out that "we are replenishing our stock" and advised, " WATCH THE DEMOCRAT-TIMES FOR OUR WEEKLY SPECIALS."

Thus, the Sam Stein store survived a critical period following the sudden death of its founder. Difficult times still lay ahead, but the potentially troublesome transfer of management to a new generation had been completed. Nevertheless, business conditions in Mississippi, and throughout the United States, remained depressed in the mid-1930s, although showing some improvement because of President Roosevelt's New Deal programs. In Greenville, the local economy benefited from the aftermath of the 1927 flood. The Army Corps of Engineers spent millions on flood repair and prevention as it straightened the bend in the Mississippi, thus diverting the river several miles west of town and converting the waters on the other side of the levee to a calm backwater called Lake Ferguson. Federal aid for rebuilding roads and for constructing a bridge across the Mississippi just south of town funneled money to the area, as did several New Deal agricultural programs that sought to reduce cotton acreage and provide government price-support loans.

During these next few years, Jake, as the oldest son, assumed the lead position in store management, although relying heavily on his brother Joe and enlisting the support of all family members to work in the business. Their sister, Sadie, had been in her first year at Louisiana State University when her father died, and she returned home to help at the store. These certainly must have been difficult times as family members sought to delineate their relative positions in the new family hierarchal structure. Fannie, a widow in her early forties and now the matriarch of the family, was by all accounts strong-willed and outspoken, described by her sister-in-law Tillie as "the boss of everything." She could be difficult and meddlesome, but Jake managed to keep the

10. Joe Stein.

store operating while at the same time learning the lessons of salesman-ship and management so critical to his future success. Already, one can detect two important components of Jake's evolving approach to how to run a successful business. First, he actively promoted the business. He didn't wait for customers to come into the store, but aggressively sought to attract them through bold promotions and frequent advertising. Sec-ond, he became active in local community activities and assumed visible leadership positions. Jake soon became an officer in both the Kiwanis Club and the Junior Chamber of Commerce. It was at one of these community functions that he met his future wife, Freda Grundfest.

Freda Grundfest had been born in Cary, Mississippi, a small Delta town between Greenville and Vicksburg. She was one of eight chil-dren—four boys and four girls—born to Morris and Molly Grundfest. Her father had been a Russian immigrant, from an area around Minsk. After coming to America, he initially settled in New York City. Her mother later immigrated to New York, most likely as part of an arranged marriage. According to family legend, when Morris went to the Ellis Island facility to meet Molly, she refused to leave with him. Morris first had to find someone that she knew, and then return to the immigration facility for that person to vouch for his identity. Only then would Molly agree to go with him. They married shortly afterwards, and then left New York. One of them had relatives in Mississippi and they traveled there, settling in Cary. At first, Morris worked as a peddler, but soon opened a country store and also tried some farming. He started with only a few acres, but began expanding the acreage used for growing cotton. The cotton farm is still in the family today, owned by one of Freda's nieces and her husband.

As a young girl, Freda never did any farm chores. She was the youngest of the eight children, and by then the family farm was well-established, with hired help doing all of the work. By the time she graduated from high school, the family had begun to scatter, with several brothers going to Little Rock, Arkansas, where they established a chain store called Sterling's, which was "what used to be called a five-and-ten." Freda attended a girl's school, Brenau College in Gainesville, Georgia, where she studied drama. Afterwards, she went to live with an older, married sister in Greenville. Freda loved drama and the theater, and the local Kiwanis Club asked her to do a recitation during one of its "Ladies Nights." In the audience that night was Jake Stein. Jake was quite taken by Freda's performance, and supposedly a friend told him afterwards, "Jake, if you don't date that girl, I'm going to break your damn neck."

Jake began courting Freda. On the surface, they may have seemed an unlikely couple—the stout, broad-shouldered, somewhat gruff, ex-jock and the petite, vivacious lover of music and the arts. But it proved a good match, and Jake and Freda married in 1935. Jake remembered returning from his honeymoon—"Joe called me into the office and said, 'Jake, you have been drawing $20 a week out of the business. In fact, you are now married and I think you can raise yourself to $25 a week.'" By the following year, two of the other Stein siblings had also married. Joe married Jane Wexler of Natchez, and Sadie married Julius Sherman, who had recently moved to Greenville from Pine Bluff, Arkansas. All of these marriages meant additional family members to support, causing "a big overhead on a little store." That undoubtedly contributed to Joe's decision to leave the Sam Stein store. In 1936, Joe opened his own store, Jay's, a more upscale women's clothing and shoe store located one block up Washington Avenue. Jake recalled that when his brother left the family business, it "relieved Sam Stein's of…two mouths to feed." Joe Stein continued

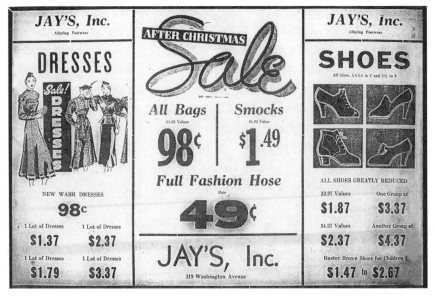

11. New Year's Day 1937 advertisement for Jay's, a store specializing in women's clothing and "alluring footware," opened by Joe Stein the preceding year.

to operate Jay's until the early 1950s, when he moved to New Orleans.

By this time, Sam Stein's had truly become a family business. Jake and his brother-in-law, Julius Sherman, worked full-time. Their wives, Freda and Sadie, also helped at the store during busy times, as did their mother, Fannie. Younger brother Bernie worked after school, and following his graduation from high school in 1937 became a full-time employee. The

12. Sadie Stein Sherman.

Stein children continued to live at the family home at 1212 Washington Avenue, with each son moving to his own home after getting married. Sadie, however, stayed at the family home after she married Julius Sherman, since as the only daughter, she would be the principal care-giver for her mother. Years later, when the Shermans moved to a new home, Fannie moved with them, and she continued to live with her daughter and family. Fannie's long-time cook and domestic helper, Ollie Bell, stayed employed by the family. After raising the four Stein children, Miss Bell subsequently helped Sadie raise her two sons, Stanley and Charles.

By the late 1930s, the family business was thriving, thus prompting plans to expand. On March 8, 1939, Greenville's daily newspaper, recently renamed the *Delta Democrat-Times,* ran the headline " Sam Stein Opens New Modern Store Tomorrow." The expansion of the store at 219 Washington Avenue involved knocking down the wall and moving into the adjacent store at 221 Washington Avenue. The expanded store would now be 125 by 50 feet, with the extra space needed "to care for the greatly increasing retail business." In addition, there would be a large 100 by 60-foot warehouse directly in the rear for the store's wholesale department. The news article included a photograph of the store's staff of nine, with Jake as the manager, Julius in charge of the shoe department, and Bernie the chief purchaser for the men's department. Sam Stein's promoted itself as "Greenville's Own Store," a place that sold dry goods, clothing, and shoes at affordable prices that working-class people in town could afford. It was the store "Where Everybody Goes, Where Everybody Saves." The new expanded store helped Sam Stein's compete in the very competitive retail market of downtown Greenville, where in a three-block area of Washington Avenue all ten of the town's principal clothing and variety stores, loosely identified in the city directory as "department stores," operated. Several of the stores were locally-owned and operated by Jewish merchants who had been in business since before Sam Stein had arrived in Greenville, such as Nelms & Blum and The Fair. Others were part of national chains, with J. C. Penney only several stores away in the 200 block of Washington Avenue and F. W. Woolworth in the 300 block.

The expanded Sam Stein's opened only six months before war erupted in Europe and by December 1941 the United States had been drawn into the conflict. World War II presented both opportunities and challenges. Military mobilization brought men and money into Mississippi, as the Army established numerous installations throughout

13. & 14. Jake and Bernie Stein during World War II.

the state. One of the largest was the Army Air Corps base in Greenville. According to one historian, "the war boom" nearly tripled the per capita income of Mississippians—although Mississippi still ranked last among all forty-eight states at both the beginning and the end of the war—"and despite wartime shortages and rationing the living standards of most Mississippians rose dramatically."[2]

While the people of Greenville and vicinity may have had more disposable income to spend, for merchants like Jake Stein the war brought additional challenges as the federal government became increasingly involved in managing the wartime economy through federally mandated wage control programs and the establishment of maximum price regulations. In May 1942, for example, Sam Stein's joined with sixteen other Greenville retail stores to purchase an advertisement in the *Delta Democrat-Times,* entitled "We Hope You Take This Scolding In The Right Spirit!" The ad pointed out that "our prices (with certain exceptions) cannot go higher than the highest prices they reached in the month of March. That means we have had to reduce the price levels on certain items." The merchants emphasized that "we're not complaining," but urged their customers to help them as "we do think it's to the advantage of this community and to our country that we stay in business. And that's where you, our customers and friends, come in. We think you ought to be willing to make more sacrifices in 'buying as usual' than you've made to date."

While Jake worked to conform the Sam Stein operation to governmental requirements and to keep customers coming into the store, he soon found himself with new responsibilities. On June 2, 1942, the City Council of Greenville elected Jake Stein, by unanimous vote, to serve on the council, replacing a long-time councilman who had died. Jake told the local newspaper, which described him as a "prominent local businessman," that he would use his $50 monthly salary as councilman to invest in war bonds. For the next eleven months, Jake took an active role as city councilman, regularly attending meetings and serving on a number of council committees that dealt with streets and sidewalks, water and public buildings, and the other mundane, but necessary, tasks of municipal governance. Finally, on April 27, 1943, Jake submitted his resignation to Greenville's mayor, as he had enlisted in the U.S. Army. Several days later, Jake left for training at Camp Shelby in Hattiesburg.

Shortly after the war started, Bernie Stein, the youngest of the family and with no dependents to support, had volunteered for the Army Air Corps. Now Jake entered the Army, and eventually served in France and Germany. After the war in Europe ended, he was a training officer involved in the redeployment of troops from the European Theater to the Pacific. With Bernie and Jake in the military, Julius Sherman, older than his two brothers-in-law, remained at home to run the Sam Stein store. In March 1946, Jake was discharged with the rank of first lieutenant. He returned

15. Freda Stein and her infant son, Jay, in early 1946.

home not only to resume his business career, but also to meet his six-month-old son, Jay.

✳ ✳ ✳

Jake returned to a Greenville that had changed, and that was on the brink of an even more dramatic transformation over the next two decades. Roosevelt's New Deal had fostered significant shifts in the Delta's agriculture-based economy through encouraging mechanization, mandating acreage-reduction programs, and promoting the use of chemical fertilizers and herbicides to increase yield-per-acre production. Labor shortages during the war years accelerated these trends. As a result, many tenants and farm laborers found themselves displaced. Some left the Delta and headed north in search of better opportunities; others moved into Delta towns and cities to look for work. Greenville and surrounding Washington County experienced significant growth. From 1930 to 1950, the population of Greenville doubled to nearly 30,000, and by 1960 would reach 41,502. Washington County had a slower growth rate, but the county's population increased from 54,310 in 1930 to 78,638 in 1960. When David Cohn returned to his hometown after the war—having stayed away for more than a decade—he noticed some subtle changes. For example, when he called the telephone operator and asked to be connected to an old friend, a long-time resident of the city, he found himself transferred instead to "Information." When he overheard people talking about "the war," it no longer meant The War Between the States, but rather the recently completed World War II. These incidents, as well as others, led Cohn to conclude, "Greenville has lost something. Its provincial charm has gone."[3]

On a more serious level, Cohn noted that those who lived in the Delta "are affected by special stresses" caused by two factors. Cohn explained, "The one is that the Delta is largely a cotton economy in a period when cotton, under attack from many sides, is a wobbly economic underpinning for the area. The other is that the Delta is a classical land of Negro settlement at a time when the attitudes of Negroes and whites toward one another are in a state of violent transition."[4] Written in 1947, Cohn's prescient observations hinted at some of the troubles that would face Greenville and the Delta and would impact Jake Stein and his business endeavors.

After his return from military service, Jake immersed himself in running the Sam Stein store and in reestablishing himself in civic and community organizations. From a merchandising perspective, one of the principal challenges facing Sam Stein's in the post-war period involved how to position itself to attract the additional prospective customers who continued moving into Greenville and surrounding Washington County. In 1948, a second, and much smaller, Sam Stein's opened in Leland, ten miles east of Greenville. Within a few years, however, this second store closed. In downtown Greenville, the principal shopping district seemed to be shifting, and two of Sam Stein's immediate competitors on the 200 block of Washington Avenue—S.H Kress and J.C. Penney—moved to new locations. With fears that "the 200 block was getting to be a thing of the past," Jake, Bernie, and Julius decided to open a new Sam Stein store several blocks away at 401-03 Washington Avenue. This new store would be managed by Bernie Stein and Julius Sherman. Jake Stein would stay at the old location to liquidate the merchandise and, if possible, sell the property.

This division of management responsibility, which initially was announced as only a temporary one, reflected deeper conflicts within the family partnership that owned the store. Prior to the war, and certainly after Joe Stein had opened his own store, Jake had been the unquestioned leader of Sam Stein's. Bernie had just graduated from high school, and Julius, while having some retail merchandising experience before moving to Greenville, had assumed an ownership position only through marriage. But the war changed the family dynamics. Serving in the military helped to mature Bernie and gave him leadership and com-

16. *Julius and Sadie Sherman, circa 1953.*

mand experiences. He left the Army with the rank of captain, and thus outranked (at least militarily) his older brother. Julius, meanwhile, earned a larger voice in managing the store since he had done so single-handedly throughout the war years while his two brothers-in-law had been gone.

The principal friction involved Jake and Bernie, who had heated arguments over operational and strategic questions, everything from the best way to advertise merchandise and promote the business to who the store's targeted customers should be. By all accounts, Bernie was emotional and hot-tempered, while Jake was stubborn and opinionated. It was not a good combination. Julius found himself increasingly placed in the role of mediator, using his diplomatic skills to keep the peace between his two strong-willed brothers-in-law. Julius evidently had honed these skills at home where he daily had to deal with a demanding and bossy mother-in-law. But these differences at the store soon spread, and even though Jake and Bernie managed to present a reasonably cordial public front, their personal relationship became more cold and formal. Jake and Freda Stein had little to do with Bernie or his new wife. After the war, Bernie had married Carolyn Levy who, as her son later recalled, had difficulties adjusting to Greenville, which she found to be an "entirely different world" from her hometown of Lima, Ohio. Instead, Jake and Freda chose to socialize with Julius and Sadie Sherman, as well as a number of Freda's Grundfest brothers and sisters.

The new Sam Stein's had its grand opening on March 16, 1950. The day before it opened, the store purchased enough advertising to fill ten pages of a special "Sam Stein Section" of the *Delta Democrat-Times*. The full-page ad on the first page of this special section thanked "our friends and customers for their loyal patronage," and offered orchids to the first five hundred women who came to the grand opening, as well as presents for the "gentlemen" and "kiddies." The promotional articles in this special newspaper section emphasized that the new store would carry only "first class merchandise," and the renamed Stein's Outlet Store at the old location would sell low-price items such as mill closeout goods, irregulars, remnants, and other miscellaneous merchandise from bankruptcies and salvage operations. According to Jake, "We feel this type of operation will bring to the people of Greenville and its trade area thrift values second to none. This will be the bargain basement of Sam Stein's."

For nearly twenty years, the two stores continued as semi-autonomous units within a family partnership consisting of Jake and Freda Stein, Julius and Sadie Sherman, Bernie and Carolyn Stein, and Fannie Stein, with the ownership percentages and profit distribution formulas periodically reevaluated. Jake had nominal responsibility over both stores, but focused his efforts on the Outlet Store, later renamed Stein's Self Service Store, or "The Big S," which sold "Nationally Advertised Goods at Ridiculous Prices." Julius and Bernie concentrated on managing Sam Stein's, with Sadie Sherman becoming more actively involved in managing the women's department, or "ladies floor." Bernie ran the men's department, with Julius responsible for shoes, piece goods, lingerie, and everything else. Both stores worked together, as necessary, to coordinate promotions, share employees, and develop complementary merchandising strategies. For example, when Jake, who had developed extensive contacts with manufacturers and jobbers from whom he purchased merchandise in bulk, found bargains that would appeal more to the upscale customer base at Sam Stein's, he would direct the merchandise there. Nevertheless, the division of the family business into two distinct entities limited the opportunities for family friction.

While Sam Stein's targeted a white, middle-class clientele by selling higher quality merchandise, Jake continued the traditional merchandising approach begun by his father. He continued to appeal to

17. Downtown Greenville looking west toward Lake Ferguson, in August 1956—Sam Stein's is at 401 Washington Avenue (arrow on left) and Stein's Outlet Store at 219-21 Washington Avenue (arrow on right).

working-class customers, a majority of whom were black. Freed from the constraints of his family partners, Jake honed his intuitive promotional instincts to increase business. As in past years, the store stocked its shelves by working with firms like New York's O'Shaughnessy Dewes and Klein, Inc. that acted as a buying agent for small retailers and specialty stores throughout the country, as well as purchasing merchandise directly from jobbers who regularly visited Greenville. Jake supplemented this standard supply of merchandise by purchasing, when possible, manufacturing overruns and out-of-season clothing, often personally visiting manufacturers and suppliers in major cities. At first, most of Jake's contacts came from St. Louis, an important market for merchants in the Deep South. Later, Jake expanded his buying efforts to other cities as well, including New York. Jake's son, Jay, remembers that as a teenager in the early 1960s his father took him to market in New York City, which he then found to be not very interesting. But he also remembers how his father had built a good rapport with merchandising reps, many of them fellow Jews—"My father developed a reputation among a group of manufacturers in New York. They loved him and trusted him. They were constantly calling with deals on merchandise for the store." Thus, Jake devoted his considerable energies to identifying large bulk quantities of closeouts and irregulars from manufacturers, and slower-selling merchandise from big city department stores. This merchandise could be purchased at very favorable prices and then sold in Stein's Self Service Store at greatly reduced prices. Bargain discount prices and big sales promotions became Jake's specialty.

While Jake tried to pursue a more aggressive discount retailing strategy during the 1950s and early 1960s, the operations of Stein's Self Service Store remained frozen in the slow-paced practices of the past. The store was long and narrow, with tables piled high with merchandise. There was no air conditioning then, only big fans set up throughout the store to keep the air moving, and Jay, as a young boy, remembers "a distinct musty odor" in his father's store. The store opened from 9 a.m. to 6 p.m., Monday through Thursday, and on Friday and Saturday stayed open two hours longer to 8 p.m. At closing time, large sheets would be placed over the show windows in front, thus preventing any passersby from watching the money being counted. When the day's receipts had been recorded and put in a bag in the safe, the sheets would come down and drop cloths would

18. *The Stein home at 1212 Washington Avenue (the number later changed to 348 South Washington Avenue) after one of Greenville's infrequent snowfalls. Sam Stein and family moved into this house in 1928. After Sam's death, Fannie lived there with Julius and Sadie Sherman and their two sons. Both Stanley Sherman and Jay Stein tell this story about Miss Ollie Bell, the family's longtime domestic helper and a superb cook of the Russian-Jewish dishes that Fannie had taught her to prepare. For years, Miss Bell answered the phone by saying, "This is Sam Stein's house." Not until the early 1960s did the Shermans (and Fannie) move to a new home. When the phone rang for the first time, Miss Bell answered , "This is Julius Sherman's house," which greatly agitated Fannie Stein.*

19. *Fannie Stein, aka "Mama Stein," outside the Washington Avenue home.*

be placed over the merchandise to keep it from getting dusty. The store closed on Sundays, but Jake worked that day as well. He generally met the porters and stock boys on Sunday mornings to work in the warehouse and restock the merchandise tables. In the afternoon, he would pay bills and do paperwork in his small office in the back of the store.

Jake had a number of non-family members as clerks, but Jay remembers the store being "a real family community." His mother,

Freda, did not work at the store often, as child-rearing responsibilities and community involvement took most of her time. But Jake was
always there, as was his mother, Fannie. Although Fannie lived with the
Shermans, she chose to work at Jake's store. Known as "Mama Stein,"
she became a "fixture" at the store, loved by customers, but feared by
employees because of her short temper. Internal controls did not exist,
and if Jake or Fannie needed $10 or $20, they simply reached into the
cash register, without leaving any documentation slip. As a result, generally only family members manned the cash register stations that guarded
the entrance and exit doors at the front of the store. Fannie, who never
did learn to read English, operated one of the cash registers, although
she frequently made mistakes and would be out-of-balance at the end of
the day. When Joe Stein suffered a fatal heart attack in the mid-1950s,
Jake left for New Orleans for the funeral, but first asked Fannie's sister
Jeanette and her husband, Bennie Davidson—who had just retired after
owning a shoe store in Greenwood—to come to Greenville to help run
the store in his absence. Afterwards, Jake talked them into staying at the
store, and they moved to Greenville, as did another of Fannie's sister,
Mary Weinberg. Thus, the store remained a loosely-run operation for
many years, with few controls other than the fact that family members
controlled the handling of cash, a not atypical management philosophy
at the time for family-owned businesses.

Outside of the family partnership that owned Sam Stein's and
Stein's Self Service Store, Jake opened several United Dollar Stores. Jake
was the sole owner, but he operated these stores in an informal alliance
with a friend, Bernard Tanenbaum, who owned some retail stores based
in Dumas, Arkansas. Jake and Tanenbaum had discussed the concept
of operating stores where almost everything cost no more than one
dollar, and they agreed that Jake would open these dollar stores east of
the Mississippi, and Tanenbaum west of the river. Beginning in the late
1950s, Jake opened United Dollar Stores in Greenville (only several
blocks from Stein's Self Service), Cleveland, and Greenwood. These
stores generally carried the lowest quality irregulars, including some
slow-moving items from the Self Service Store, and appealed to an even
poorer, almost exclusively black, customer base. West of the Mississippi,
Tanenbaum and his son expanded this concept into a chain of nearly
300 stores that they sold to Dollar General Corporation in the late

1970s. But Jake focused his efforts on the Self Service Store, and never gave that kind of attention to his dollar stores. Also, Jake never placed a lot of emphasis on inventory management and other basic controls, which made running a multi-location retail operation very difficult. The United Dollar concept only proved profitable in Greenville, and even there, in the early 1960s, Jake had to fire the manager for stealing. He then hired an old family friend, Monnie Rosenthal, who had just retired as manager of a Top Value Stamp Redemption store. Rosenthal managed Greenville's United Dollar Store for the next fifteen years, and when he finally retired in his early eighties, Jake closed the store.

In addition to managing his part of the family business, Jake found time to become one of the leading power brokers in Greenville's business community. He invested his energy in numerous community endeavors, and a listing of his civic involvement is impressive. He served as president of the Kiwanis Club and the Greenville Community Fund. He was a member of the board of directors of both the YMCA (Young Men's Christian Association) and YMHA (Young Men's Hebrew Association). When an attempt was made to bring minor league baseball back to town, Jake became president of the Greenville Bucks of the Class D Cotton States League. And the list could go on, although Jake's friends would have been quick to point out that many of his charitable activities went unpublicized as he quietly provided money, clothing, and other assistance to needy families in the community.

Jake became a tireless worker in the on-going efforts to attract new businesses and industries to Greenville, an economic necessity given the dramatic changes in the region's agriculture-based economy which faced a decline in farm labor jobs caused by increased mechanization and a decline in the importance of cotton relative to new synthetic fibers. During the post-war years, Greenville opened an industrial park and aggressively sought to attract companies involved in metal products, concrete, timber, and the processing of farm commodities. The city expanded its harbor and port facilities, thus attracting numerous towing and marine repair companies. For years, Jake played an active role in these business development activities through his involvement with the Greenville Industrial Foundation and the Chamber of Commerce.

Jake served as president of the Chamber of Commerce beginning in 1950. During his term as head of the organization, the Chamber engaged in one of its most important business development campaigns, an effort to convince Alexander Smith & Sons Carpet Company to open a new carpet manufacturing plant in Greenville under Mississippi's Balance Agriculture With Industry (BAWI) program. Under BAWI, local municipalities could issue bonds, use the proceeds to build an industrial facility, and then rent it to a company at a rate sufficient to retire the bonds in twenty years. Jake played a key role in the courting of Alexander Smith & Sons, negotiating with the company's management, while simultaneously promoting the passage of a $4.75 million bond issue that was the largest bond commitment approved up to that time under the statewide program. This successful campaign promised to bring approximately 900 new jobs to Greenville, with an annual payroll of $2 to $3 million. And the impact of the new manufacturing plant increased even more when, a few years later, Alexander Smith & Sons moved its corporate headquarters from Yonkers, New York, to Greenville.

While Jake certainly played a highly visible role at the Chamber of Commerce, he also worked behind-the-scenes. As in most communities, Greenville had an informal group of leading businessmen who utilized their influence in subtle ways to shape business and municipal priorities. Jake was one of them, on close terms with Hodding Carter, the influential Pulitzer Prize-winning publisher of the *Delta Democrat-Times*, and other key business and civic leaders. For years, Jake belonged to an informal group that every afternoon met at the Downtowner Hotel to drink coffee and to discuss, among other subjects, ways to get things done that would benefit the community. Bob Harding, one of his coffee group buddies and a friend of more than forty years, summarized Jake's influence: "I've never seen anyone as generous with his time and efforts, and his material things. He was active in the community, in just about everything that there was. He was just a man that there are not any like anymore. He was frightfully concerned with everything that went on in the community."[5]

While Jake involved himself in civic affairs from a businessman's perspective, his wife Freda approached community service from the standpoint of drama, music, and the promotion of the cultural arts. During her first years in Greenville, Freda appeared in a number of Little Theater productions. She later took a leading role in the Delta Music Association that sponsored visiting concert performances and became president of that organization. She chaired the Red Cross blood bank and worked for the local March of Dimes. When their son, Jay, reached school age, she became active with his school activities and president of the PTA (Parent-Teacher Association). Freda and Jake Stein became what would later be called a "power couple," both well-known throughout Greenville and vicinity for their commitment and dedication to improving their community.

The Steins also held leadership positions within Greenville's Jewish enclave of several hundred families. Jake served as president of the Hebrew Union Temple for three years in the late 1940s, and his brother-in-law, Julius Sherman, and brother Bernie (and years later, Bernie's son Robert) subsequently took their turns as president of the synagogue. Jake remained an influential member of the congregation. He chaired local fundraising campaigns for the United Jewish Appeal, and later the sale of State of Israel bonds. Freda was president of the Sisterhood at the Hebrew Union Temple and for a number of years chaired the Temple Sunday School. For the Steins, as well as other Jewish families in Greenville, the synagogue became an important center for their spiritual and social lives. Nevertheless, Greenville Jews, as was true of Jews throughout the South, had to make modifications in traditional religious practices to accommodate the Christian majority. They accepted the realities of not having kosher food readily available and not being able to close their stores on the Sabbath, since Saturday was the busiest shopping day of the week.

Greenville's Jewish community remained the largest in Mississippi, although by the mid-1950s fewer than 2,500 Jews lived in the entire state. Throughout the South, enclaves of Jewish settlement could be found, but none were large. Southern Jews faced occasional prejudice and social discrimination, but seldom suffered violence in a region with a history and reputation for savagery and brutality. The 1915 Georgia lynching of Jewish businessman Leo Frank, described as "America's most horrifying example of antisemitism,"[6] remained an isolated, albeit well-remembered, incident. What antisemitism existed generally involved little more than rhetoric, usually directed against what one historian described as "the shadowy, imaginary Jew who lived far away in the big cities," not the few Jewish families who lived nearby.[7] Since Jews made up such a small proportion of the population throughout the South—only about one-half of one percent—they did not appear threatening, especially when compared to the large number of blacks, who were in the words of Jewish writer Eli Evans "the lightning rod for prejudice." As Evans observed, "If economic competition with immigrants was a major cause of antisemitism in the North, Southern fears were too focused on the threat from Negro advances to worry about the few Jews there. Whatever else one can say about gentile attitudes toward Jews, Jews are considered white men first and live most of their lives as part of the white majority."[8] In fact, a number of contemporary southern writers—including Greenville's own William Alexander Percy—believed there to be far greater anti-Catholic hatred than anti-Jewish prejudice.[9]

Among Southern towns, Greenville historically may have been among those most free from religious intolerance. The Ku Klux Klan—which hated Jews and Catholics almost as passionately as it did blacks—had never established a foothold in Greenville. When the KKK made a determined effort to organize a local unit in the early 1920s, former U.S. Senator LeRoy Percy, the most influential of the wealthy landowners who dominated the local power structure at the time, successfully opposed them. Over the years, the political and civic leadership of Greenville—from the Percy family to the editors of the local newspaper, Hodding Carter, and later his son, Hodding III—fostered a community spirit of religious toleration. Writing in *The Atlantic* in 1948, David Cohn commented, "In Greenville neither I nor any of my coreligionists, to my knowledge, suffered any indignity or lack of opportunity because of being Jewish…. There were bigots in the town, it is true—Jews as well as Gentiles—but they were a tiny minority looked upon commiseratingly by the majority as unhappy aberrants."[10] Certainly in Greenville, there existed no more antisemitism than one might find elsewhere, including in the North. As Freda Stein later recalled, the community leadership consisted of both Jews and non-Jews, and you could not tell one from the other except during the holidays "when everyone got real religious." But in 1954, and in the years that followed, this tolerant attitude became strained.

Everything changed on May 17, 1954, the day that the United States Supreme Court issued its landmark decision in the case of *Brown v. Board of Education*. By a unanimous nine to zero vote, the Court ruled segregated public schools unconstitutional, thus reversing the doctrine of "separate but equal" that had been institutionalized nearly sixty years earlier. The court ruling was condemned throughout the South, where all elements of white society—from government officials to the poor, lower-class "rednecks"—vowed resistance to all efforts aimed at ending segregation and the regional social customs that kept blacks in a second-class status. This backlash against the Supreme Court decision, and the ensuing civil rights controversy that lasted for more than a decade, caused consternation among Jews.

In many areas of the South, Jews had tried to keep a low profile while attempting to assimilate into Southern society, hoping to be simultaneously both Southern and Jewish. One historian, who set out to discover what it meant to be a Jew living in the South, concluded, "Jews did not want to stand out in society. They did not want to appear different from other Southerners. They wanted their own Reform temples to seem just like another Southern church. And they fretted constantly lest some Jew make an untoward remark, or take an unpopular stance on a public issue, which might bring the whole Jewish community into disrepute."[11] An important facet of this acculturation involved the quiet acceptance of the regional consensus concerning segregation. While Southern Jews, in many cases, may have had more enlightened views about race relations than their Christian brothers, they rarely spoke out against the status quo. The Supreme Court decision, however, focused unwanted attention on Southern Jews because of the prominent role that Northern Jews played in the NAACP and other civil rights groups and the well-publicized Jewish support—both financial and intellectual—for integration. Thus, the actions of their coreligionists in the North raised suspicions about the motives and loyalties of all Jews. Under these circumstances, the racist, bigoted attitudes that Southern whites held toward blacks could be transferred readily to other individuals and groups that might not support the regional consensus on segregation.

Nowhere did the Supreme Court decision result in a more bitter or violent reaction than in Mississippi, where blacks made up 45 percent of the population, the largest percentage of any state in the country. This backlash came at a time when Jake Stein, then in his mid-forties, had begun to reshape his family business, Stein's Self Service Store, into the largest and most heavily promoted department store in the entire Delta.

The story of Jake Stein and what would become Stein Mart cannot be told without placing it in the larger context of the racial tensions and violence of the 1950s and the civil rights movement of the 1960s that transformed society not just in Mississippi, but throughout the United States.

For Jake Stein, as well as other merchants and store owners, the troubles that followed *Brown v. Board of Education* made managing and promoting their businesses more challenging. Local merchants depended upon the good will of their fellow townsmen, who also happened to be their customers. Even in the best times, merchants had to be careful not to antagonize those who patronized their stores. To further complicate matters, Jake, like his father, had directed his merchandising efforts toward working-class customers. According to his son Jay, Jake followed a very simple retail philosophy—"My father's theory was to attract people into the store through price—moderate merchandise at a budget price. So consequently, because of that, we would have a mixed clientele, from the top society of Greenville on down." Although the Stein store catered to both white and black customers, Jay estimated "it was predominantly black." Blacks felt comfortable shopping at Sam Stein's, and later Stein's Self Service, because Jake treated them with respect, as Sam had done before him. And the Steins showed a willingness sometimes to negotiate on the price of merchandise, which black shoppers liked. For years, Greenville had had a reputation for maintaining the best race relations of any town in the Delta, or in all of Mississippi, so this mixing of white and black shoppers had never before caused any problems. But with the heightened tensions in the decade that followed 1954, extra caution would be required to maintain the good will of both white and black customers, while simultaneously ensuring that all of the unwritten racial conventions of the day were followed.

One of the first responses to *Brown v. Board of Education* was the establishment of the White Citizens' Council to oppose desegregation. The first Council originated in the Delta town of Indianola in July 1954, and within a year it had spread to most counties in Mississippi. What made the White Citizens' Council so intimidating was that membership came not from the lower-class, less-educated rednecks so often associated with the Ku Klux Klan, but instead from local bankers, merchants, government officials, and the "respectable" elements of society. Failure to cooperate with the Council could be devastating. As one Jewish storeowner complained, "The money dried up at the banks and loans were called in. If you had a restaurant, linen wasn't picked up; if you owned a store, the local police could play havoc with you on the fire laws."[12]

The White Citizens' Council movement led to the establishment of decentralized local and state associations, with considerable autonomy, throughout the South. While the Citizens' Councils of America, the nominal coordinating organization, officially disavowed violence, the rhetoric and intimidation practiced by local Citizens' Councils stifled the right to free speech and dissent and tended to legitimize violence, as numerous individual Council members became implicated in the beatings and murders that became ever more frequent occurrences. Council leaders repeatedly insisted that the organization was not antisemitic, although some of the most ardent segregationists among its membership harbored anti-Jewish sentiments. When interviewed for the documentary film *Delta Jews,* Jay Stein remembered the Citizens' Councils as "a glorified businessman's Ku Klux Klan." Expressing views that certainly reflected those shared by his father, Jay continued, "They didn't ride horses, with hoods on. They walked down the street with a suit and tie on. Their feelings were not quite as radical, but they were pretty tough. They clearly did not believe in the equality of man. And they probably didn't like Jews a lot more than they liked blacks."

To counter the antisemitic undercurrents often found in its literature and occasional statements from members, the Citizens' Council published a pamphlet entitled, "A Jewish View on Segregation," supposedly written by an anonymous Jewish Southerner. The pamphlet claimed that Jews could join the White Citizens' Council and in doing so would ensure no antisemitism. The pamphlet continued with a not-so-subtle threat—"So the Jew who attempts to be neutral is much like the ostrich. And he has no right to be surprised or amazed when the target he so readily presents is fired upon."[13] A number of local Citizens' Councils solicited Jews to become members, and often Jewish businessmen found it easier to pay the three- to five-dollar annual fee than to face the possible economic pressures that they feared from any refusal to go along. Whether or not to join the White Citizens' Council became a subject for debate among Greenville Jews, especially after one of the more prominent Jews in town quickly associated himself with the organization and encouraged others to follow his lead. Jake Stein resented the Citizens' Council and refused to join. He urged others not to give in to the Council's intimidation tactics. According to the recollections of Hodding Carter III, Jake's leadership proved critical during a heated meeting at the Hebrew Union Temple to discuss whether or not the synagogue should endorse the White Citizens' Council. According to Carter, "Jake was not a confrontational man, but he never backed away from tough issues."

Another foe of the White Citizens' Council, which established a local Council in Greenville that first year, was the editor of the *Delta Democrat-Times*, Hodding Carter. In March 1955, a prominent national magazine, *Look*, published Carter's harsh assessment of the Citizens' Council, entitled "A Wave of Terror Threatens the South." In response, the Mississippi House of Representatives overwhelmingly voted to censure Carter for having "lied, slandered...and betrayed the South." In Greenville, the Citizens' Council held a public meeting to denounce the *Delta Democrat-Times* and its editor/owner. It urged merchants to boycott the newspaper. Jake Stein refused. Years later, he told Carter's biographer, "They came in and asked me to stop advertising in the *Democrat-Times* and I said I couldn't stay in business if I didn't advertise."[14] Jake probably told the Citizens' Council representatives much more than that, since he regarded them with the same scorn as he did the Ku Klux Klan, but these more forceful and colorful comments have not been preserved.

For the next decade, Hodding Carter, and later his son Hodding III who succeeded him as editor, used the pages of Greenville's *Delta Democrat-Times* to fight the White Citizens' Council and to preach the need for peaceful solutions to the state's racial troubles. The elder Carter enjoyed enormous prestige and a national reputation, having won a Pulitzer Prize a decade earlier for his editorial writings advocating racial and religious tolerance. Carter was by all accounts a "Southern moderate," more enlightened and tolerant than most of his contemporaries, but nevertheless it must be noted—as several historians of the civil rights movement have done—that he favored only a gradual dismantling of the region's racial caste system. He may have been, as biographer Ann Waldron described, "as brave as a kamikaze warrior, year after year writing articles and editorials that attacked racism and discrimination."[15] Nevertheless, Carter did leave behind a wealth of writings, not only newspaper editorials but also a prolific number of books and magazine articles, to illustrate that he thought "separate but equal" represented the best approach for Mississippi to follow, at least in his lifetime. He repeatedly denounced the NAACP and other civil rights organizations and did not support the desegregation of public schools and other facilities. As a result, one critic has called Carter just a "fair play segregationist."[16]

These criticisms are unfair, as Carter probably pushed his advocacy of tolerance and equal economic (as opposed to social) opportunity as far as he could, and still remain in Mississippi. One must remember that Mississippi in the 1950s and 1960s was a scary place, and there are numerous accounts of the horrific consequences of violating, or even questioning, the accepted status quo. For blacks, it often meant brutal beatings or death, with no chance that the local courts would convict the perpetrators; for whites, it meant ostracism, threats, and eventually exile. One of those who did openly challenge Mississippi's demand for conformity in the defense of white supremacy was University of Mississippi history professor James Silver, who wrote, "Within its own borders the closed society of Mississippi comes as near to approximating a police state as anything we have yet seen in America."[17] After the publication of *Mississippi: The Closed Society*, Silver had to leave the state, where he had lived for twenty-eight years, to teach at Notre Dame.

Jake Stein continued to be a friend and staunch supporter of Hodding Carter. Whether Jake's views on segregation and civil rights differed from those of his friend will never be known because, unlike Carter, Jake left behind no written documentation. What is certain is that Jake and a number of his close business associates were among the local civic leaders who, working with Hodding Carter, helped to set the tone for what happened in Greenville and vicinity. Greenville was in the heart of the Mississippi Delta, a region where blacks comprised approximately 70 percent of the population. There existed a clear and direct correlation between the percentage of blacks in an individual community and the intensity of the opposition to desegregation and the likelihood of violence. And no place in the South was as violent as the Delta, where towns such as Greenwood, Cleveland, and Belzoni became synonymous with violence and brutality. But not Greenville. In the voluminous literature detailing these frightening times in Mississippi, whether from journalists sent to the state, or from Northern college students and civil rights activists who headed south, or from

20. *The 200 block of Washington Avenue, with Stein's Self Service Store located between Fred's Discount Store and Mullins. Three years after this 1961 photo, Jake Stein bought all of the stores on the 200 block of Washington Avenue so that he could undertake a major expansion of his store.*

later historians, Greenville receives little mention. Whatever underlying tensions might have existed, Greenville remained peaceful and quiet. And for that, Hodding Carter, Jake Stein, and other local business and civic leaders who worked quietly behind-the-scenes, deserve credit.

Racial tensions and the intransigence of white segregationists reached their highest point in 1964 and 1965 as civil rights activists, who only had begun protesting in Mississippi several years earlier, now came to Greenville. These demonstrations, peaceful and certainly less confrontational than in other nearby Mississippi towns, coincided with Jake Stein's plans for a major expansion of his Stein's Self Service Store. In early April 1964, Jake announced that after nine months of planning and negotiations, he had acquired all of the property along the south side of the 200 block of Washington Avenue, including Mullins Credit Store, Bernie Brill's second-hand clothing store, and several vacant, deteriorating buildings. Jake planned to triple the size of his existing fifteen-thousand-square-foot store by knocking out the interior walls of several of these adjoining buildings and renovating the enlarged space. Several other buildings on the west side of the block would be demolished to build a one hundred and thirty-five-car parking lot for customers. Jake promised expanded clothing and houseware departments, as well as new merchandise such as an appliance department that would carry everything from air conditioning units to refrigerators. Jake estimated that renovations would be completed by September or October. The *Delta Democrat-Times* applauded the proposed "radical transformation of over half a block of downtown business property" and expressed hope that "it could be the signal for similar downtown business renovation as customers are attracted to the area."

Within weeks, Jake began promotional sales, advertising in bold letters that "Stock Must Be Sold Before Big Expansion Program Gets Underway," and promising that "'Big S' Low Prices Slashed Even Lower!" In his own enthusiastic prose, Jake announced, "Soon hammers will swing—walls will come down—dust will fly and we will be on our way to bringing you Greenville's Greatest Store. We must make room for our work crew. Here is the beginning of our great selling spree." Thus began more than six months of huge promotions, with large, often full-page ads several days a week proclaiming "Great Expansion SALE." After the first month, one should have surmised that Jake was not simply cleaning off the shelves, because merchandise kept coming into the store as fast as he could sell it. And advertisements that almost screamed "Our Contractors Are Yelling…'We Need Room'" and "The Last Wall Is Coming Down.…We're Selling It At Cost!" just kept the promotional sales machine going.

While Jake supervised the expansion and remodeling of his store and conducted one big sale after another, Mississippians found themselves overwhelmed by the events of the summer of 1964. In Washington, Congress debated, and eventually passed, landmark civil rights legislation that prohibited discrimination in public accommodations, strengthened voting rights statutes, and set up procedures to guarantee

21. Washington Avenue as photographed from the U.S. Post Office Bulding in an attempt to get a panoramic view (circa 1965). Sam Stein's is on the left at 401 Washington Avenue. In the middle of the 300 block is the Sterling variety store, part of the chain owned by Freda Stein's brother, Dave Grundfest.

equal job opportunities. Black activists organized the Mississippi Freedom Democratic Party to compete with the all-white state Democratic organization and sent its own rival slate of delegates to the national convention where it challenged, unsuccessfully, the credentials and party loyalties of the regular delegation. Meanwhile, hundreds of civil rights volunteers, mostly white students from Northern colleges, came south to participate in the Mississippi Project of 1964, more popularly known as "Freedom Summer." Sponsored by the Council of Federated Organizations (COFO), a coordinating entity for a coalition of the Student Nonviolent Coordinating Committee (SNCC) and three other national civil rights organizations, the volunteers set up and staffed "Freedom Schools" and community centers for blacks at forty-four project locations and conducted voter registration drives to encourage and assist blacks to register to vote.

In Greenville, the number of Freedom Summer volunteers fluctuated from thirty-five to more than one hundred during the two and

one-half months that the program lasted. In late June, as volunteers began arriving, the local COFO spokesman told the *Delta Democrat-Times* that their efforts would emphasize voter registration and warned that COFO was "prepared to push to the limit with these demands." The newspaper also reported that the local police chief, although hopeful that there would be no trouble, had taken the precaution of briefing all policemen on possible riot procedures. But over the course of the next several months, little happened in Greenville, especially when compared to the arrests, beatings, and general lawlessness that occurred in Jackson, Greenwood, McComb, and other cities. The disappearance in June of three volunteers, Mickey Schwerner, Andrew Goodman, and James Chaney—two New York Jews and a Mississippi black—and the discovery of their murdered bodies six weeks later entombed in an earthen dam, created a national outrage that prompted Justice Department intervention in the state. One study of the civil rights struggle in Mississippi concluded that "the summer of 1964 was the most violent since Reconstruction."[18] COFO compiled a detailed listing of "hostile incidents" that grew to twenty-six mimeographed pages. It alleged one thousand arrests, eighty worker beatings, thirty-seven church bombings, and other violent acts, but only eight "incidents" occurred in Greenville, none very serious.[19] As the Freedom Summer volunteers began to head home, the *Delta Democrat-Times* referred to the last several months as "The Long Cool Summer" and opined that "all Greenville citizens can be proud of what happened and what did not happen while the COFO project was underway."

With a majority of the COFO volunteers leaving town, Jake Stein worked feverishly to get his new, expanded store ready, as construction delays pushed its opening back to mid-November. During these last few months of remodeling activities, Jake's brother-in-law, Dave Grundfest, visited Greenville. Dave and his late brother Sam had started the Sterling Stores in Little Rock, Arkansas, in the years following World War I, and the variety store chain had grown to eighty-five outlets in six states, including one in downtown Greenville. Eager to show off his new store to his brother-in-law, Jake gave him a tour of the in-progress construction where this amalgamation of distinct, separate buildings were being

22. This April 1964 advertisement is one of the first in a series of advertisements during the next six months announcing huge sales during the construction of the new Stein Mart store.

23. The new Stein Mart store.

gutted and transformed into a single, giant shopping area. During this inspection visit, Dave Grundfest asked Jake what he planned to call the new store. Jake hadn't decided. Grundfest then told him about a fellow in Arkansas named Sam Walton who a few years earlier had opened a discount store called Wal-Mart. He suggested that Jake call his new store Stein Mart.

After the end of business on Sunday, November 8, Jake closed Stein's Self Service Store for the final time. The store remained closed for three days, while Jake and his staff prepared for the grand opening of the new store. On Wednesday, November 11, he purchased eight full pages of newspaper advertisements, inviting everyone to "Come See…the Delta's newest and largest one-stop DOWNTOWN DISCOUNT CENTER," and announcing drawings to give away a free television, portable dishwasher, and other prizes. The next day, as the new parking lot filled and a crowd of shoppers waited for the 9:30 opening, the name of the new store, emblazoned in large, distinctive script letters across the front of the new facade, read "Stein Mart." And that same distinctive Stein Mart lettering is still in use today, nearly forty years later.

The new block-long Stein Mart store was like nothing Greenville had ever seen, and the newspaper reported that "thousands" of shoppers came that first day. In addition to expanded selections of clothing, linens, fabrics, and other merchandise that had always been carried, and priced at deep discounts, new departments sold auto accessories, electrical appliances, refrigerators, and sporting goods. It was one-stop shopping, from toothpaste and hair spray to record players and televisions. Jake also introduced Stein Mart's own credit card, and the sales staff encouraged shoppers to fill out applications for the "Stein Mart Charge Account." The opening created so much excitement in the Greenville area that a photo of Jake in the new store and an article about the opening, "New Life Surges In Downtown Area," made the front page of the *Delta Democrat-Times*.

With the opening of Stein Mart, Jake Stein stood on the threshold of his greatest merchandising successes. During the next two decades, he would further refine his merchandising strategies and continue to operate a tremendously successful local Greenville business, one that soon became the most well-known store in the entire Mississippi Delta. But one disturbing cloud hung over Stein Mart, and all of Greenville, as 1965 began, and that was the increasingly strident tone of the civil rights workers who remained in Greenville. By this time, COFO had begun to unravel because of internal dissensions among the four civil rights organizations that temporarily had joined forces. Consequently, COFO became increasingly dominated by SNCC, the most radical of the civil rights groups. In Greenville, the COFO/SNCC remnant joined forces with a new group, the Delta Ministry, which under the sponsorship of the National Council of Churches had set up a field office the previous fall. Thus, as the civil rights activities of 1965 unfolded, a more fragmented but much more radical-dominated group demanded changes in how Greenville did business.

Troubles started in January 1965 with demonstrations and picketing at the Greenville Mill, the large carpet manufacturing plant that Jake Stein had helped to recruit to the city a decade earlier. The demonstrators protested alleged racial discrimination at the plant and demanded that more blacks be hired and given better-paying jobs. These demonstrations continued for months, and soon protests about discriminatory hiring and promotional practices spread to other businesses in town, as well as to the city's school administration building and the county hospital. As a result, local businessmen, under the sponsorship of the Greenville Chamber of Commerce, began discussions on how to respond. In early May, the Chamber unanimously approved a resolution, endorsed by businesses throughout the city, that the "Civil Rights Act of 1964 is the law of the land and must be obeyed." The resolution called on local businessmen to offer "employment opportunities" and "reasonable advancement to all qualified persons without regard to race, color or creed." At the same time, a group of twenty-nine "Negro Greenville organizations" issued a second resolution expressing their views concerning equal job opportunities. But neither the Delta Ministry nor COFO expressed any support for these resolutions, instead intensifying their protests and announcing plans to file various lawsuits in federal court.

Stein Mart had been one of the local businesses that endorsed the Chamber of Commerce statement. Jake had for years employed blacks in his store for cleaning, maintenance, or stock work, but never in customer service or cashier roles. Now he hired two blacks as trainees to learn how to operate the cash registers, and promised to hire another black cashier later in the year after he completed an expansion of his shoe department. The Delta Ministry complained that hiring these new employees did not go far enough, and its leaders opened negotiations with Jake by demanding that half of the workforce be black. Only the year before, Jake had significantly expanded his staff to accommodate his larger Stein Mart store, and to now comply with the Delta Ministry demands would force him to fire a number of employees who had done a good job. Jake refused. During the past several months, there had been occasional demonstrations outside of the Stein Mart store, but in early July the Delta Ministry began picketing out front every day from 9 a.m. to 9 p.m. to protest what they called Stein Mart's "consistent failure to negotiate in good faith." At first, the protesters acted aggressively, stopping passersby to hand out leaflets calling for a boycott and blocking the entrances to the store. That first day, the city police arrested ten people, and thereafter the protesters, under close watch by the police, proved less belligerent. Picketing and efforts to get black customers to boycott the store continued throughout the summer.

The picketing angered Jake, as well as his family and friends, and also hurt him. Jay, home from college that summer, remembers, "It broke my father's heart. Here was someone who had done so much for the town, so much for members of the black community. In came a bunch of folks from out-of-town. They thought that they had a purpose and felt they could accomplish that purpose, in great part, by damaging the merchants downtown." Since Stein Mart was the largest store downtown, it became the logical target, with no consideration given to whether or not Jake, or the Stein family business, had been good friends to the local black community over the years. Nearly forty years later, Jay still becomes agitated over the memory of that time—"I just remember all day long, ranting and raving. Marching and chanting. Singing and cheering. And we had an empty store as a result of it. Not totally. We had some loyal supporters during that time. We had a lot of them. But our black clientele was afraid to cross the picket line. They [the demonstrators] would have cameras, with no film in it, and play like they were taking pictures of people who went in the store. It was a tragic, tragic time for my father. It wasn't much of a payback for him."

The decision to target Stein Mart also angered many in the Greenville community. The leader of one group of local blacks publicly complained that those out-of-towners making decisions for the Delta Ministry should consult with local people first, and his group withdrew its support for the civil rights coalition. The *Delta Democrat-Times* had never looked favorably at the Delta Ministry, previously questioning "whether they are not in truth more interested in destroying the community than in helping to build it toward true unity, racial harmony and progress for all." Now the Carters used the editorial pages of their newspaper to defend their friend Jake Stein, charging that the protesters have "now degenerated into irresponsibility of the lowest order. In choosing to picket—and boycott—the Stein Mart, their faction has revealed itself as only a small cut above the level of common gangsters." The editorial equated the economic pressure trying to be asserted against the Steins to "the same kind of thuggery in which the Citizens Councils once engaged." A month later, as the boycott continued, the *Delta Democrat-Times* carried another editorial deploring that "a great wrong is being perpetrated under false banners," and expressed outrage that more local black leaders, while privately opposing the boycott, had not spoken out. Pointing out that Stein Mart had been "a leader, not a laggard, in seeking to break the old color barriers," it continued, "the bitterest irony of the whole affair is that those Negroes who are diverted from the Stein Mart, as much through ignorance of the facts as through support for the picketing, often go instead to a nearby store which has steadfastly refused even to consider hiring Negroes."

Despite the protests, and the poisonous atmosphere that now filled downtown Greenville, Jake tried to pursue "business as usual." Throughout the summer, he continued to advertise regularly to let the community know that Stein Mart remained open for business, and still offered deeply discounted prices on all merchandise. He negotiated a deal with Name Brand Discount Shoes to operate the store's shoe department on a leased basis, and then added an additional 3,000 square feet to the rear of the store—which enlarged the entire store to nearly 50,000 square feet—for this new shoe venture. In early August, just in time for back-to-school shopping, the store hosted the "Grand Opening" for its four separate shoe departments—men's, ladies', children's (all three with brand-name shoes), and "ladies budget shoes." The opening festivities included a visit from Name Brand's president, former Ole Miss and New York Giant quarterback Charlie Conerly, who greeted customers and signed autographs. Ever the promoter, Jake Stein worked hard to ignore the unpleasantness of the picketing demonstrators outside and to concentrate on the merchandising and selling that he so enjoyed.

By the fall of 1965, the protests in Greenville faded, as they did throughout most of Mississippi. There would still be some loud demonstrations and occasional violence during the next several years, but the dark days of brutal repression to protect the regional orthodoxy of "segregation forever" had passed. These had been difficult times for Jake Stein, as a community leader, as a respected businessman, and as a family man. Now, in the late 1960s, he could turn his full attention to managing his business and grooming his son to succeed him.

24. Jay Stein in 1979, the year after he became president of Stein Mart.

CHAPTER 3

The Young Visionary

"Yet the story of Jews in the South is the story of fathers who built businesses to give to their sons who didn't want them. It is a drama played over and over again thousands of times across the South. My father was typical — he had wanted to go to law school but his generation was caught by the Depression and trapped into a business the immigrant generation started, a business that he merchandised into a success during the war and the years that followed.... Neither my brother Bob nor I found it easy to break away, because we suffered under the tensions of a beckoning family business while perceiving widening opportunities in the North."

– Eli N. Evans, *The Provincials:
    A Personal History of Jews in the South.*

*A*s the acrimony over desegregation peaked and the struggles among Mississippians intensified over how to reconcile their society to changing social and racial norms, the mid-1960s saw a new challenge confront the Stein family partnership. By the 1960s, the third generation of Steins — the grandchildren of Sam Stein — were coming of age. Did any of them have the desire to continue in the family business?

Small family-owned businesses have always faced the problem of management and ownership succession. Does the next generation wish to follow in their parents' footsteps and keep the business in the family — and, if so, do they have the personal leadership qualities and the business management skills necessary to do so successfully? It is a theme repeated over and over, and often so privately and quietly that small family businesses fade away with little fanfare and scant remembrance that they ever once thrived.

This issue became especially pronounced for Jewish merchants in the South, as the younger generation — especially during the civil rights problems of the 1950s and 1960s — perceived that greater opportunities could be found outside the region. In the early 1970s, Eli Evans, who had chosen to become a writer rather than a merchant, surveyed the condition of his coreligionists who lived in the South, a region where "Jews languished as the provincials, the Jews of the periphery, not destined to triumph but just to survive."[1] He found that many of his contemporaries had made the same choice as he had, abandoning the South and the family business. His father, Emanuel J. "Mutt" Evans, had taken over a small store in Durham, North Carolina, owned by his father-in-law and had grown it into a chain of six stores, with hopes that he and his two sons could expand into every major city in the state. His oldest son chose instead a career in broadcasting, and then Eli — soon to start his junior year at the University of North Carolina and fearful of being "channeled into the store to live a life of compromise" — told his father that he also did not wish to be part of the family business. One detects some feelings of guilt as Evans recounts, "The implications for the family were clear enough. It had taken forty years to build the business; it would take just a little while to sell."[2]

Sam Stein had died too young to know any of his ten grandchildren. But few of this third generation had much interest in retailing, or in staying in Greenville. Joe Stein had left the family business years earlier when he opened his own store, Jay's. Joe closed his store and moved his family to New Orleans in the early 1950s, in part to manage the estate of his wife's family and in part because New Orleans had better schools for his daughter, Emily, and son, Joe Jr. After Joe Stein suffered a fatal heart attack in August 1956, his widow and children remained in New Orleans. Joe Jr. later became an investment banker in New York City.

Sadie and Julius Sherman had two sons, Stanley and Charles. As the first grandchild, Stanley was the favorite of his grandmother Fannie, who lived in the Sherman's home. In high school, an automobile accident left Stanley's legs paralyzed, but that did not prevent him from working at both family-owned stores, although restricted to the back offices because of the difficulty maneuvering his wheelchair through the narrow aisles of the sales floor. After graduating from the University of Mississippi and then completing a year and a half of law school, Stanley returned to Greenville in late 1963. For more than twenty years, he worked off-and-on at the stores, often spending his mornings at Sam

Stein's and his afternoons at Stein Mart, counting the cash receipts and doing some bookkeeping. After the formal division of the family business into two separate corporations, Stanley became secretary-treasurer of Sam Stein, Inc., although that official position did not preclude him from continuing to work for his Uncle Jake. But Stanley quite openly expressed his dislike of the retail merchandising business, and his bookkeeping work for the two stores was more of an informal part-time sideline to his other interests. In 1970, Stanley and several friends opened a bar, and he later got involved in managing and owning radio and cable television stations. While Stanley had little interest in the family business, his brother Charles had none. Charles was very studious and loved to read. His parents sent him to prep school in New England, and then to Columbia and New York University Law School. He became a New York City lawyer and, except for occasional family visits, never returned to Greenville.

Bernie and Carolyn Stein had five children — four daughters and a son, Robert — but all of them were considerably younger than their Stein and Sherman cousins. In the late 1960s, when decisions about the family business and ownership succession issues needed to be addressed, Robert was only in prep school, attending Admiral Farragut Academy in St. Petersburg, Florida. Whether or not any of Bernie's children would show enthusiasm for a retail merchandising career remained uncertain, although subsequent events would indicate only sporadic interest. In the mid-1970s, after graduating from Mississippi State University, Robert did work at Sam Stein's for several years before moving to California to work for a department store chain. He returned to Greenville in the mid-1980s and again worked for the store for several years before becoming an insurance salesman. Neither Robert nor his sisters Nancy and Judy, who struggled when asked to manage the women's department for several years after Sadie Sherman's death, appeared to have any strong commitment to retailing, although Robert subsequently would own and manage a men's big and tall clothing shop for more than a decade. Thus, neither the children of Julius Sherman nor Bernie Stein seemed destined to carry on the merchandising legacy of the family.

Only Jay Stein, the only child of Jake and Freda, showed any real interest in the family business. Growing up, Jay worked at the store after school and on weekends, as his father and uncles had done before him. Jay had great admiration and respect for his father and wanted to emulate him. Looking back and reflecting on why he decided to pursue a career at the family-owned Stein Mart, Jay recalls, "I enjoyed the business, or what I thought the business was to be. I enjoyed Greenville back then. I felt it was the sort of place where I could create a life. It really was the only business I ever felt comfortable in and knew…. It was not back then a very complicated business. I saw how my father did it, and I thought I could do it a little better, a little bit differently."

Jay had been born on September 14, 1945, in Greenwood, Mississippi. When Freda was pregnant, her physician had moved to Greenwood, so when the time grew close for her delivery, she went to Greenwood, the town where Jake had been born and where her mother-in-law still had family. Jay has fond memories of his early years in Greenville, which he remembers as "very warm, very loving, very embracing." Growing up in a small town gave him "a sense of place." Even though the backlash against desegregation caused difficult times during the 1950s and early 1960s, Jay does not recall any problems, or at least none that affected him, as Greenville really had "separate societies — whites over here, and blacks over here."

Jay also appreciated Greenville's "close-knit," supportive Jewish community — "I got a sense of family from that community, a sense of belonging, and a sense of spirituality. It was very much a part of my life — Sunday school, parties, my parents' friends. It gave me a sense of who I was, a sense of what it meant to be Jewish. It had nothing but positive influences on me." Jay also had lots of family nearby. He enjoyed the Shermans and was friends with both Stanley (who was six years older) and Charles. He felt especially close to his mother's family, finding his Grundfest relatives to be "less complicated than the Steins." He saw three of his Grundfest aunts "all the time," and they all spoiled him. He became very close to his Aunt Sadie and her husband, Bill Klaus, who lived in nearby Cary. They had no children of their own, and Jay considered them "my second parents."

When it came time for school, Jay attended kindergarten at St. Joseph Catholic Church, located on the block next to the synagogue. His mother has saved the mimeograph graduation program, which illustrates Greenville's well-known reputation for religious tolerance as Father Maloney awarded diplomas to Jay and to Jerry Hafter and Benji

25. Jay Stein at age 13, when he was attending public school in Greenville.

Nelkin, the young sons of two other prominent Jewish residents. Jay then attended Carrie Stern Elementary School and remained in Greenville's public school system through his sophomore year in high school. By the summer of 1961, Jake and Freda had decided to send their son to an out-of-state preparatory school. The escalating rhetoric and violence associated with the desegregation crisis, and the resulting anxieties and vulnerabilities felt by many parents throughout Mississippi, certainly contributed to the decision. Friends had recommended The Bolles School in Jacksonville, Florida, and Jay started there in September 1961. By his own admission, Jay had not been a great student and needed a more disciplined approach to his studies. At Bolles, Jay's academic performance improved. He joined the debate team, became assistant editor of the school newspaper, and played on the varsity golf team. But Jay remembers that "Bolles was not a particularly happy experience for me," especially his first year when it was still a military school.

After graduating from Bolles in 1963, Jay chose to attend New York University because its retailing major offered a five-year program with a co-op plan that allowed students to attend class and also gain practical work experience. At NYU, he enrolled in internship programs to learn about both the retailing and manufacturing sides of the business, working two years at Saks Fifth Avenue and two years at Union Underwear, which manufactured the Fruit of the Loom brand. Jay did not finish NYU's program, instead returning home to work in his father's store. He later regretted not completing college, admitting "that was a mistake, in retrospect, but I was very anxious to come home and begin my career."

Jay had enjoyed working in his father's store while in school and during summer vacations, but returning in the summer of 1967 to work full-time and to be groomed for taking over the business proved more difficult than anticipated. Jay had ideas about how to make the business better, and he wanted to incorporate some of the lessons learned at college and during his internships. But Jake was set in his ways and had little interest in changing how he operated the business. Jake provided little formal guidance to Jay and failed to define clear areas of responsibility for his son. To Jay, it seemed that his main job was simply "to do what my father didn't want to do."

From Jake's experience, running a successful retail store meant spending time on the sales floor, greeting customers, listening to them explain what products they wanted, and ensuring that they received good service. He could always be found on the sales floor, except when meeting with traveling sales representatives or when new shipments of merchandise arrived at the warehouse in back of the store. Then Jake would rush to the warehouse to "bust open" the boxes and start to price the new goods. He had a phenomenal memory for what merchandise he had bought and how much he had paid for it, plus an intuitive sense of how much his customers would be willing to pay. So the pricing of new merchandise depended less on formal invoices or other paperwork, and more on instinct. The new merchandise would be rushed to the sales floors and piled high on the counters. One long-time employee remembers that when first hired she tried to straighten and fold the clothes, only to have Jake come along and mess up everything on the table. Jake then told her that piles of merchandise attracted customers, who enjoyed sorting through stuff thrown together in a heap. Jake always carried a black pen, and if he saw merchandise that was not selling as fast as anticipated, he would on-the-spot scratch out the old price and write in a new one, without ever worrying about formally recording the price changes or markdowns.

Recognizing customer service to be a critically important component of running any successful business, Jay thought there must be more to retailing than spending twelve hours a day in the warehouse or on the sales floor. He believed that some of the haphazard, seat-of-the-pants operational procedures had to be improved and that Stein Mart should consider some new strategic alternatives. Jay advocated the development of formal guidelines to monitor inventory and keep track of markdowns, and he recommended that some basic auditing procedures be put in place. These improved controls would be needed

26. Freda and Jake Stein, 1973.

before considering expansion beyond the Greenville store.

Jay also thought that the store should upgrade the quality of its merchandise. He wanted to continue his father's discount pricing strategy, but favored offering a wider selection of merchandise, especially higher-quality, name-brand clothing, linens, and other "soft goods." He later succinctly summarized his ideas as "wanting to sell steak at hamburger prices." Jay and his father had quite different ideas about fashion. Jake always had favored basic, common clothing, with the most important considerations being whether or not it fit and how much it cost. He cared little for fashion himself, and almost every day wore dark blue pants, a short sleeve white shirt, and a sweater vest. In the words of Hodding Carter III, he looked like "an unmade bed." Jay, on the other hand, took after his mother, and shared her interests in art, music, and fashion. Jay dressed stylishly and developed a flair for recognizing fashion trends.

Jake gave little encouragement to Jay, and the two of them would battle — sometimes in loud shouting matches on the sales floor at Stein Mart — over Jay's suggestions. To Jay, his father's unwillingness to consider new ideas surprised him. Jake always had been highly respected among local Greenville businessmen. For years he had been a director of one of the town's leading banks, Commercial National Bank, and after its acquisition had been named to the board of the acquiring bank in Jackson. Other businessmen in town would seek his advice. While Jake "would be very forward-thinking when it came to other people's businesses," Jay found that not to be true when his father focused on his own business. "His advice was well sought-out, all over town. He was thought of, clearly, as one of the most successful people in town. But our business — as successful as it was — was still a very small-town, family business that lacked more structure that I wished it had."

The conflicts between Jake and Jay reflected some painful father-son dynamics at work. Jake had limited parenting skills, patterned almost inevitably after those of his own father. He always had been a workaholic, preferring the store to home. Jay remembers that growing up, he seldom saw his father unless he went to the store. Friends and employees described Jake as gruff and stern, and observed that he did not smile often. They also described him as a big-hearted, generous person, with a real empathy for those less fortunate than himself. Stories of how Jake helped others, especially poor black families in Greenville, are numerous. If he saw a family in the store that he knew to be down on its luck, he would ask what they needed and how much they could afford to pay, then adjust the price of the merchandise so that they could buy it. When the house of one black family that regularly patronized the store burned, he gave everyone in the family new clothes. Unfortunately, Jake had difficulty showing these same qualities of warmth and kindness to his own family, whether battling with his brother or failing to spend quality time with his son.

As Stanley Sherman would later observe about his uncle's workaholic ways, "Jake had a harsh mistress." Unless involved with some civic or community activity, Jake could always be found at work, from early morning to late at night, seven days a week. He had no hobbies, and what little free time he had, generally on a Sunday afternoon, he spent playing poker with buddies at the YMHA or watching football games on television. It is little wonder that when Jay sought advice as a teenager, or later needed a loan for a down payment on his first house, he went not to his father, but to his uncle, Bill Klaus.

For seventeen years, from 1967 until Jay moved the company headquarters away from Greenville in 1984, Jay and Jake battled over one thing or another. Jay hoped to prove himself and sought affirmation from a father he respected. Jake initially resisted Jay's ideas and recommendations, sometimes ridiculing his son's suggestions, and then only begrudgingly agreed to give them a try. He seldom spoke a good word to Jay, even when these new initiatives proved successful, although when Jake would get together with his coffee group "he would burst the buttons off his shirt bragging about what Jay had done." One observer of these father-son battles recalls, "Both of them were very strong personalities. I have seen them fight like cats and dogs…but they loved each other fiercely."

One area of disagreement that Jay and his father resolved quickly, and with a minimum of bitterness, involved the structure of the Stein family partnership. Even before he returned from college to work full-time, Jay had felt uncomfortable with the arrangement that involved Sam Stein's and Stein Mart being operated autonomously, but with the profits from the two entities pooled for equal distribution to the family partners. Jay thought the partnership agreement inequitable, with his parents receiving the short end. Not only did the new Stein Mart have a much higher volume of sales than did the Sam Stein store, but Jake promoted his store more aggressively and effectively. In Jay's view, there existed two very different operating philosophies — "My father was more aggressive than the rest of his family in getting business. Other members opened their doors and said, 'Please come.' My father opened the doors and made sure they came."

Jake found it difficult to address the issue of formally separating the two stores. Even though he had frequent disagreements with his partners at the Sam Stein store, he always had done business within the family context. But Jay remained insistent, and received the crucial support of his mother. The fact that none of the other cousins seemed interested in the family business only strengthened the case for dividing the company. But how could the split be accomplished? Bill Tarver, the family's accountant, proposed a plan that would keep the two stores interconnected, but allow for an ownership redistribution. Under Tarver's proposal, Jake and Freda would get three-fourth ownership of Stein Mart and one-fourth of Sam Stein's, and Bernie and Julius and their wives would get one-fourth of Stein Mart and three-fourths of Sam Stein's. Since Stein Mart had become the larger and more profitable store, Jake had to come up with some additional cash to pay for the difference in equity. Eight or nine years earlier, Jake had invested in a towboat company, and he now sold his interest in that venture and used part of the proceeds to pay Bernie and Julius. This arrangement proved to be merely an interim step, and several years later the two stores incorporated as separate entities, with Jake in sole control of Stein Mart, Inc.

While splitting the Stein family business happened with relatively few problems, Jay's efforts to establish better management systems met with less enthusiasm. Everyone who knew Jake Stein recognized that he was a great merchant in the sense of knowing what merchandise to buy, how to negotiate the best price, and how to advertise and promote his business. But he had no interest in operational issues. Jake ignored the need for improved financial or inventory controls, even though the expansion and enlargement of Stein Mart several years earlier had increased the complexity of his operation, with additional employees hired to staff the larger store and several of the new departments outsourced to third-party companies. Family monitoring of store operations — which had been the key control mechanism for decades — just did not work as well. The family control of the cash register stations no longer proved feasible, as sales volumes increased after the 1964 Stein Mart opening and the energy levels declined for Fannie Stein and her generation of family employees. In the late 1960s, Fannie was diagnosed with cancer, and her working days at the store became more limited prior to her death in 1971. Nevertheless, Jake insisted on continuing to operate with minimal paperwork and controls, depending instead upon his incredible memory for the merchandise purchased and sold, as well as his intuitive sense of knowing when something in his store just did not seem right.

Efforts to modernize Stein Mart's operations would be a slow process. Jay did convince his father to hire a company that specialized in operational audits for retailers, and the preliminary report from these efficiency experts indicated a need for tighter controls. Although reluctant to move forward with many of their recommendations, Jake agreed to hire an experienced manager to run the operational side of the store.

They chose Clyde McGee, who years earlier had been a schoolmate of Jay's and previously had worked for the Kroger Company in Greenville. He instituted the first limited controls, for example the use of void slips when cashiers made mistakes on the cash registers. He remained manager of the store for about five years, and then Claude Beck replaced him. Both McGee and Beck concentrated their efforts on making small improvements in operational efficiencies and managing day-to-day staffing issues. However, not until the late 1970s, with the opening of Stein Mart's second store in Memphis and the hiring of the company's first controller, Clayton Roberson, did Stein Mart begin to make any real progress in modernizing its operations.

While Jay tried to get his father to pay more attention to management issues, Jake shared his merchandising expertise with his son. Jake took Jay with him to trade shows and to visits with manufacturers and other retailers. He spent these years introducing Jay to the many contacts that he had made among manufacturers and suppliers and demonstrating his strategies for negotiating the purchase of large quantities of merchandise at the most advantageous prices. During one of these trips in the early 1970s, they met Emil Moos, a senior executive with Saks Fifth Avenue. Moos had responsibility for disposing of Saks's surplus merchandise, including those clothes and accessories that had not sold by the end of the season and those that had been returned by customers. Saks had a very liberal return policy, and most of the returned merchandise would be in excellent, almost new condition. All of this merchandise would be boxed and sent to a warehouse in Yonkers. Negotiating to purchase this Saks merchandise was an art, as the warehouse was stacked high with boxes, with neither identifying labels nor any consistency as to what would be found in each box. Jake went though the warehouse, put his fist through some of the boxes to get an idea concerning the contents, and then offered Moos so much per box based upon that sampling. This first encounter between Jake and Emil Moos proved a success — they became great friends, and Stein Mart became the principal outlet for surplus merchandise from Saks Fifth Avenue for more than a decade.

Emil Moos was to be a key figure in Stein Mart's development. He had emigrated from Nazi Germany in the 1930s and had started out working at Gimbels sweeping floors, gradually working his way up

the ranks into the executive staff of the corporation that owned both
Gimbels and Saks. Moos took a liking to Jake and Jay. He became an
informal advisor to the two of them and, after his retirement from
Saks, a consultant for the company. Jay considers Moos to have been
not only a friend but also a mentor, one who played "a tremendous
role — both personally as well as professionally — in my growth." In
the years ahead, Moos would be consulted on key issues facing the
company, providing sage counsel as well as helping to arbitrate differences between father and son. And he continued to supply the Steins
with Saks surplus merchandise, knowing that they would sell it at
deeply discounted prices but also realizing that none of Saks's regular
customers would ever know because Greenville, Mississippi, was about
as far from New York City as you could get.

In Greenville, Jake priced the Saks merchandise — an eclectic collection of formal dresses, name-brand clothing, imported handbags
and shoes, and unique gifts and knickknacks — at deep discounts
of 50 to 75 percent off, and sometimes even more. Dresses and coats
that Saks might sell for $1000 or more would be priced at $100. These
"Saks Sales" proved enormously successful, and within several years
these semi-annual events attracted people not only from the Mississippi Delta but from other nearby states. They came to Greenville for
the bargains, plus the festive atmosphere and excitement generated
by the sales, which generally lasted several weeks or until all of the
merchandise had been sold.

At first, the "Saks Sales" were held in the Stein Mart store, with the
merchandise displayed in a special area at the back. Hundreds of shoppers would gather outside in the morning, waiting for the store to open.
As the hour approached, employees received warnings to keep out of
the aisles, instructed instead to stand behind the pillars or in the safety
of the cash register stations. Once the doors opened, Clayton Roberson
remembers, "There was a mad dash. People screaming, throwing things,
kicking, [and doing] whatever they could do to get back to that area,
just to start digging through those tables of merchandise."

One year, the surge of the crowd when the doors opened pushed
some customers through the plate glass windows in the front of the
store. Several people were cut, but they still ran down the aisles,
while bleeding, looking for bargains. After that incident, Jake real-

27. & 28. Scenes from a Saks sale in Greenville.

ized that he needed to move the sale out of the main store. He first leased a store one block away in the 300 block of Washington Avenue. This building allowed more sales space to be used, and the extra room was needed as Jake began supplementing the Saks merchandise with closeout and end-of-season purchases from Nordstrom, Neiman-Marcus, and other department stores. Not only did he use the annex location for the "Saks Sales," but in the months between the sales he kept it open as Stein's Salvage Store, in some respects a replacement for the United Dollar Store that had closed several years earlier. Merchandise that had not sold well or that had been damaged or returned, whether from the Stein Mart in Greenville or from one of the stores that Jay opened in other cities, would be sent to the Salvage Store. After Sam Stein's closed in early 1988, Jake leased that building from Bernie and Julius, and he moved the Salvage Store to that location.

Stein Mart®

SEMI-ANNUAL
SAKS FIFTH AVENUE
SALVAGE SALE
CONTINUES

SUNDAY STORE HOURS
1 TO 5:30

WE HAVE STOCKED OUR STORE WITH
MERCHANDISE FROM SAKS AND SOME OF OUR
OTHER STEIN MART STORES

WE ALSO HAVE SOME SAKS JEWELRY

SAKS FIFTH AVENUE FASHION
PRICED LOWER THAN EVER!

- DESIGNER AND FAMOUS NAME FASHION
- MEN'S AND LADIES' SHOES
- FABULOUS ACCESSORIES
- DISTINCTIVE GIFTS AND LINENS
- PLUS MUCH, MUCH MORE!

ALL SALES ARE FINAL. NO EXCHANGES OR RETURNS.

STEIN MART | Company Clearance Center
...AT 401 WASHINGTON AVE.

(THE FORMER SAM STEIN BUILDING - WASHINGTON AVENUE & SHELBY)

29. 1993 advertisement for the semi-annual Saks sale, to be held at the Stein Mart Clearance Center, formerly Sam Stein's at 401 Washington Avenue.

The "Saks Sales" became, within only a few years, the retail bargain events of the year. At first, some of the locals didn't know what Saks was, and even asked if they should bring their own "sacks" to carry their merchandise. All of Stein Mart's employees have stories to tell, and they all remember the stampede of customers as the doors first opened. One of them compared it to "cows coming to eat." Others recall how people would grab large armfuls of merchandise and then pile it on the floor, where they claimed possession by sitting on it. Sometimes, the shoppers would work in teams, with one guarding their pile of clothing, while others searched for more. As noon approached, one of the team would go out for lunch and bring back food for the others to eat while leisurely sorting through their pile of potential bargains. Some women would wear leotards so that they could strip off their clothes in the middle of the store to try on merchandise. Customers occasionally would try to sell merchandise from "their pile" to other shoppers who had not been so quick in staking their claims. Fights would break out. Eventually, Stein Mart hired special security guards to supervise the shoppers and settle disputes.

These stories, when first told to those who had never been to one of Greenville's "Saks Sales," may seem too outlandish and exaggerated to be true. In 1989, however, one of Stein Mart's executives, Larry Shelton, videotaped the spring and fall sales held at the former Sam Stein store at 401 Washington Avenue. It is like nothing you have ever seen. There is a huge, boisterous crowd gathered outside the store as the head of "security" explains the rules that must be followed and the unacceptable behavior that will get shoppers arrested. Then there is the mad rush into the store, with entire racks of merchandise disappearing in the first frenzied moments. Amidst a constant din, excited shoppers stand shoulder-to-shoulder — whites and blacks; rich and poor; well-dressed and jean-clad — maniacally pawing through the piles of clothing and shoes looking for that special bargain. It is an unforgettable spectacle.

There have been no "Saks Sales" since the mid-1990s, but they are still talked about in Greenville, and many wish that they would return. The Stein Mart organization of today is in many respects a very different one from when Jake Stein launched his first "Saks Sale" in the early 1970s. But these extraordinary sales events may best define Jake's merchandising and promotional genius. Jake sold quality merchandise, at deeply discounted prices, and he made these bargains available on an equal basis to all of his Greenville neighbors. The sales took place in a festive, fun, exciting atmosphere. Jake would want to be remembered that way.

✴ ✴ ✴ ✴ ✴

In the mid-1960s, Jake Stein had had a dream of building something bigger and better. He wanted to take his successful but relatively small store that primarily sold work clothes, dresses, shoes, other basic clothing, and fabrics, and make it into a super-sized variety discount store. By expanding his range of merchandise to include appliances, automotive accessories, and other goods and by offering more extensive selections of clothing — most of which he would continue to purchase as closeouts and end-of-season bargains to keep his costs low — Jake hoped to attract customers not just from Greenville and its immediate vicinity, but shoppers from throughout the Delta. With his flair for merchandising and his commitments to maintaining deeply discounted prices, Jake had succeeded beyond all expectations, transforming Stein's Self Service Store into Stein Mart, a regional retailing success story. Now, in the mid-1970s, his son Jay had a vision for once again taking the family business in a new direction.

By 1977, Jay Stein had worked with his father for a decade, still trying to make changes and improvements in how Stein Mart operated. "I've always enjoyed fashion," Jay recalls. "I've always thought that I had an eye for merchandise. Back then, I wanted to prove myself and carry merchandise in the store that was beyond what we carried — a little bit better, a little bit higher quality, a little more expensive." But Jake remained opposed to making any changes that might in any way jeopardize the successful retailing formula that had a proven track record in Greenville. He himself had little interest in fashion, and he doubted that most of his Greenville customers did either. But that year, Jake did agree to give Jay an opportunity to try out some of his ideas — not in Greenville, but in Memphis, Tennessee.

There appear to be two reasons why Jake finally gave his son the go-ahead for a second store. First, in 1977 Jay married Cindy Greener, and Jay felt that being married "gave me more credibility with him." Second, Jake had grown tired of Jay's insistence on trying new approaches, and he thought that the best way to silence his son would be to let him try and watch him fail. Jay remembers driving to Memphis with his father, mother, and Cindy and discussing what they should name the new store. Jake suggested "Fifth Avenue Brands" or just "Stein's," but he didn't want it called Stein Mart, fearing that it would be a "dismal failure." Jay insisted on calling it Stein Mart. His father finally agreed, but only after receiving assurances that the new store would be organized as a separate legal entity. Jay believed that his father's attitude reflected "him not having confidence in me," and that made Jay even more determined to succeed.

Memphis had been selected simply because it was the closest big city to Greenville. One Sunday, Jay and his father drove there for the day to look for a suitable site. Neither being very familiar with Memphis, they drove around the city in what Jay compares to "looking for a needle in a haystack, and not really knowing what a needle looked like made it even worse." They finally stopped at the home of Herbert Lichterman, a friend of Jake's who owned a successful shoe business. After they told him their plans, Lichterman said he knew the perfect location and took them to a strip shopping center on Summer Avenue where one of the retail spaces recently had been vacated by the Parks-Belk department store. Lichterman knew the center's owner and phoned him to come show the building on a Sunday afternoon. It had 35,000 square feet, but Jake wanted to put up a wall through the middle and only lease half. Jay wanted the whole store, and that became "the first of many, many opposite views that we would take." Ultimately, Jay prevailed and they rented the entire store.

The next challenge involved finding a manager for the new Memphis store. Prior to becoming manager of the Stein Mart in Greenville, Claude Beck had worked for Shainberg's, a junior department store with some 200 small shops throughout the mid-South. The Shainberg's operation had fallen on hard times and recently had been acquired by a St. Louis-based retailer, the P. N. Hirsch Company. As a result, many of Shainberg's managers had begun looking for new jobs, and Beck suggested that the Steins talk with Carl Davis, a former Army paratrooper and Vietnam veteran, who had worked for Shainberg's for nearly ten years and now managed one of their Memphis locations.

Acting on Beck's recommendation, Jay called Davis and asked him to come to Greenville. Davis agreed, meeting Jay at his home and then visiting the Greenville store. Initially, Davis was not favorably impressed, finding Stein Mart "more like a dollar store type environment." After Davis returned to Memphis, Jay called him again. When Davis told him of his reservations, Jay responded that he had some different ideas for what to do at the proposed store in Memphis, and invited him for another visit. On Davis's second trip to Greenville, Jay explained his plans for "discounting, but on a different level." Davis now became more enthusiastic and when Jay mentioned that he needed two men, Davis recommended a young Shainberg manager who a year earlier had worked for him as an assistant, Larry Shelton. Two weeks later, Davis and Shelton drove to Greenville and met with Jay and Cindy, as well as Jake and Freda. Shelton remembers walking through the Greenville Stein Mart — which was approximately 50,000 square feet, nearly five times the size of a typical Shainberg's — and being "overwhelmed more by the store than anything else. It was huge and bustling with customers. It was an entire city block." Sensing that they stood on the threshold of an exciting new business venture, both accepted jobs with the Steins, Carl Davis as manager of the new Memphis store and Larry Shelton as assistant manager.

Less than two months remained to get the Memphis store ready to open. Jay, with his father's help, began making arrangements for large shipments of clothes from several major New York retailers. Davis and Shelton began scrambling to find fixtures and employees. The Steins sent some old tables and hanging racks from their United Dollar Store, then in the process of being closed, and gave them $100 to look for additional fixtures. "That was probably the toughest thing that we did," Davis recalls. "We went begging and borrowing. We could find used racks, but we never bought a new fixture for that store. We would find racks that had no bars on them. So we would go to the junkyard and buy metal bars. We'd come back and hacksaw them, put them onto the fixtures, and clean them up the best we could…. It was a real mishmash. None of the fixtures matched."

Davis and Shelton started hiring for the nearly forty full-time positions. About half the people who showed up for interviews were former Parks-Belk employees, and they hired a number of them. Also, a lot of new hires came from Shainberg's, including four out of the five full-timers who had worked at the store that Shelton had just

30. *Advertisement in the* Memphis Commercial-Appeal *announcing the September 8, 1977, opening of Store No. 2 in Memphis*

left. The new managers relied heavily on their Shainberg experience, because they received little supervision from Greenville as they worked to put the new store together. Time sheets, refund pads, and the other everyday paperwork necessary to become operational had a familiar Shainberg look.

In the days leading up to the September 8 grand opening, Stein Mart began running ads in the *Memphis Commercial-Appeal.* Hardly anyone in Memphis had ever heard of Stein Mart, but advertisements claiming 40 to 80 percent off on new merchandise from well-known New York department stores Saks Fifth Avenue and Bonwit Teller attracted notice. As the new store began stocking its sales floor, it had a

31. March 1978 advertisement for a "Saks Fifth Avenue Sale" at the Memphis store. According to Carl Davis, these so-called "Saks Sales" of close-out merchandise were held during the first several years in Memphis, but were much smaller and less frenzied than the ones in Greenville. Note the sun rising in the corner of the advertisement, with the message, "See what tomorrow will bring." Jay Stein especially liked this advertising slogan. He explained, "The purpose of that ad was, 'Every day will be different. If you miss a day at Stein Mart, you'll miss something. See what tomorrow will bring.' The problem with that was that nobody thought that the advertising was for today, but for tomorrow."

more limited product scope than the Greenville store — no appliances, no sporting goods, no health and beauty aids, no lunch counter. But in accordance with Jay's plan, it would be, despite the shabby look of some of the hastily assembled fixtures, more upscale. From the front, women's clothing would be on the right side of the store, and men's clothing on the left, with linens down the middle. Fabrics and rugs were in the back, with a small gift department just inside the front door. When the doors finally opened at 10 a.m. on Thursday, September 8, Jay and his wife and parents stood on the mezzanine at the back of the store and watched hundreds and hundreds of shoppers rush in.

And the customers kept coming, lured by continuing newspaper advertisements announcing quality goods at discounted prices and by word-of-mouth advertising about fantastic bargains and great customer service. One customer in those first days who was not pleased was Emil Moos. He had encouraged Jay in his plans to expand to a second location, and he flew to Memphis to see the new store. Carl Davis picked up Moos at the airport and drove him to the store. Getting out of the car, Moos stared at the front of the building, where two huge banners flanked the Stein Mart sign, each proclaiming in bold letters "Merchandise From Saks Fifth Avenue and Other Fine Retailers." Moos got red in the face, turned around, and with his usual "militaristic bearing" began walking backward toward the store. When Davis asked what was wrong, Moos responded, "I'm going to pretend that I didn't see those signs." Once inside the store, Moos found Jay, and the two of them went into the small manager's office on the mezzanine for a discussion. The signs soon came down.

Within a few weeks, the success of the Memphis store — especially in the women's and men's clothing areas — created a new problem. The store began running out of merchandise. Jay had been so busy preparing for the opening of the store that he had neglected to develop a formal plan to replenish the inventory. The new, more upscale concept for the Memphis store required a steady inflow of merchandise, and not such a reliance on "opportunity buys" and end-of-season or surplus purchases. So Jay flew to New York City to meet and negotiate with different manufacturers. While in New York, Jay met Phil Dobuler, an experienced jobber who had worked in the New York fashion district for nearly twenty-five years. Jay had just completed the purchase of some Givenchy blouses when the manager of the clothing company introduced him to Dobuler. When Jay mentioned that he had gotten everything he needed on this buying trip except silk dresses, Dobuler immediately called a friend who had 1500 silk dresses for sale. Jay bought them all, and soon began to rely on Dobuler — first on a commission basis, then on a monthly retainer — to help identify purchasing opportunities for upscale ladies' clothing. Jay and Phil became for the next several years Stein Mart's New York "buying team." Jay remembers, "What he didn't have in merchandising skills, he had in personality and a Rolodex. He knew everyone in the market. Whenever or whatever I needed, if he didn't know him, he would know him ten minutes later."

Jay began to devote more and more effort to developing stronger relationships with manufacturers, especially those who made designer clothes. To make his upscale discounter concept work, Jay wanted to get more merchandise directly from manufacturers, thus reducing his dependence on purchasing end-of-season and returned merchandise from larger department stores. Jay needed a steady supply of current, fashionable merchandise, but many manufacturers expressed unwillingness to deal with an "off-price" retailer or discounter because of problems that might result if a full-scale department store sold the product at one price and a discount store down the street sold that same product at 50 percent less. This problem is illustrated by an incident that Carl Davis remembers. The owner of a successful men's shop in Helena, Arkansas, visited the Memphis store. He had attempted to branch out by opening an exclusive ladies' shop, but it failed. Now he hoped to sell his inventory, and to do so below cost. Davis introduced the man to Jay, who asked if he carried Izod shirts, then a very popular brand, in his men's shop. The store owner answered that he did. Jay then offered to buy the entire ladies' inventory at the price quoted, with no haggling, provided that the man also sell him, at cost, 100 dozen Izod shirts. Several weeks later, after the shirts had arrived, Davis received a visit from Izod's regional sales manager, who told him he didn't care how Stein Mart had acquired the shirts, but he had come to offer "full retail price for all of the Izod merchandise to get it off our shelves." Thinking of the windfall profits to be made by this transaction, Davis called Jay in Greenville. When informed of the offer, Jay told Davis to throw the Izod sales manager out of the store. Jay explained that he had no interest in selling the shirts for a quick profit, but instead he wanted to build a reputation with his customers for having better quality merchandise.

Jay still worked closely with his father in purchasing merchandise for both stores, but each was looking for something different. Even though they had different taste levels, Jay had learned well the art of negotiating and building a network of contacts. He constantly looked for opportunities to purchase current, top-line goods and targeted several major designers. He tried to make inroads with Ralph Lauren for several years, but had no success because it was difficult for a small operation in Greenville and Memphis to get noticed. When negotiating to purchase some sell-off merchandise from Garfinckel's in Washington, D.C., Jay

32. Carl Davis in the manager's office on the mezzanine of the Stein Mart on Summer Avenue in Memphis. With Davis is Pam Smith, the first head of the ladies department at the Memphis store.

got to know the manager of its men's department. He previously had worked for Ralph Lauren, and he made some phone calls to introduce Jay to several people at the company. Through these contacts, Jay began purchasing Ralph Lauren clothes, at first in relatively small quantities. Since Stein Mart did not have any stores in big cities, "we were under the radar screen" and no one complained about these designer clothes being sold at discount prices. As the purchase of Ralph Lauren clothing increased, it opened important entrees not only to customers, but also to other manufacturers of upscale and designer clothes. In Jay's estimation, "If any one connection that we ever made has to do with the success of our company, it's the Ralph Lauren one.... Ralph Lauren was the first major designer for men. The uniqueness and rarity of having his goods twenty years ago was just tremendous. We'd get shipments in and it would be gone in one day."

Jay used his considerable negotiating skills to purchase these Ralph Lauren clothes and those from other manufacturers at lower prices than the large retail chains and specialty stores paid, thus allowing Stein

Some of our Best Shoppers are our Competitors.

The next time you come into Stein Mart, don't do a double take if you see _____ of _____ or _____ of _____ shopping in our store. Fear not, your eyes are not deceiving you, but alas our competitors are shopping Stein Mart. Now admittedly, they are not our most profitable customers, but it is nice to see that they recognize quality. The thing they do not recognize, however, is our price. It is a lot different from theirs.

But that's Stein Mart. We love the fact, we brought an alternative in quality shopping to Memphis. Our customers love that alternative, too. And that's a fact.

So to our retail competitors, we are sorry you have to come way over to Summer Avenue to see our prices, but you see if we were located close to you we would have to charge your prices. Then there would be no Stein Mart, and a lot of people would be unhappy, mostly ourselves.

HAPPY THANKSGIVING

33. This November 1979 advertisement in the Memphis Commercial-Appeal *poked fun at its competitors, claiming that they too shopped at Stein Mart because of the quality merchandise and low prices.*

Mart to sell the merchandise at a substantial discount and still make a profit. Jay did this by not insisting on some of the financial concessions that the large retailers routinely required. He did not ask for advertising allowances, return privileges, or mark-down reimbursements if the merchandise didn't sell. Plus, Jay showed a willingness to negotiate the purchase of end-of-season and leftover goods as part of a package deal that included current merchandise.

While Jay focused on expanding and upgrading the merchandise, Carl Davis worked to make the Memphis store successful. With ladies' clothing being the fastest selling merchandise, Davis enlarged that department and shifted it more toward the center of the store. He moved "designer fabrics" and other home decorating goods to a separate Home Décor Center in the same strip shopping center, with his wife, Inge, as manager. She catered to home decorating firms, and gave professional decorators an additional discount to shop there. Although the Home Décor Center produced more than $1 million in sales its first year, it had a major drawback in that customers could not leave the main store with their other merchandise — until they had already paid — to walk down the shopping center to look at fabrics or related home decorating items. Consequently, when the Summer Avenue store expanded in August 1981 by leasing an adjacent storefront and tearing down the adjoining wall, Davis moved the home decorating merchandise back to the main store.

Davis emphasized customer service. He instituted special approaches to make the shopping experience a memorable one, and one that would motivate customers to tell their friends about how well they had been treated. Davis had a rule that if a customer was in the process of purchasing a lot of merchandise, the salesperson should call him or Larry Shelton. For example, if a man was buying five or six suits, Davis would come to the sales floor, be introduced to the customer, and then pick out five or six ties to give to the customer for free. If a woman was making a large purchase and it was getting close to noon, Davis would meet the person and invite her to lunch, compliments of Stein Mart. Davis kept a list of high school students to call in case it rained on Saturdays. He would give each a large umbrella and instructions that, when a customer drove into the parking lot, one of the students should go out to the car with the umbrella, greet the customer, and then escort her back to the store.

This level of service, coupled with aggressive newspaper advertising, continued to bring affluent shoppers to the store, even though there remained a stigma attached to shopping at a discounter. Davis remembers many times in those first years seeing prominent people come into the store, and look around to make certain that no one there knew them. Then, after purchasing merchandise and leaving the store, they would take the items out of their Stein Mart bag and put them in another bag so that no one would know that they had shopped at a discount store. "I personally observed," Davis recounts, "over the years that change from a furtive shopping trip to bragging about 'Look at what I got at Stein Mart!' That change took place before my very eyes. People that had plenty of money would brag about how much they saved at Stein Mart — 'I saw the same thing at Goldsmith's for $20, and I got it for $15.'" And nothing reinforced this changed perception about Stein Mart more than the introduction of the "Boutique Ladies."

The "Boutique Ladies" concept had its origins in Greenville, where Jay had invited the wives of his friends to work at the store during "Saks Sales." These women found the sales atmosphere exciting, and, best of all, they had the same opportunity as the regular Stein Mart clerks to get the first look at the Saks merchandise and to purchase items with an additional employee discount. Shortly after the Memphis store opened, Jay began to refine this idea, and the concept evolved into one where affluent, society women worked one day a week, waiting on customers in a special fashion-oriented department and calling their friends to tell them about new designer clothes and accessories that had arrived in the store. The Boutique concept became an integral part of future Stein Mart stores as the company subsequently expanded. In 1992, the *Wall Street Journal* ran a front-page article about the Boutique Ladies who "share a flair for fashion and a practiced vivacity that draws their friends and other well-heeled customers" to Stein Mart. Jay told the *Journal* that the Boutique Ladies were "our secret weapon."[3]

It somehow seems fitting that Jake Stein, by all accounts a promotional genius, will be remembered for his "Saks Sales," a high-energy frenzy as shoppers stampeded through the aisles of his store, grabbing for merchandise and brawling for bargains. By contrast, Jay will be remembered for developing a program that recruited cultured and affluent women with a flair for style and fashion not only to shop at Stein Mart, but simultaneously to work as part-time employees and to encourage their friends and social acquaintances to shop there as well. And it all started in Memphis.

The first Boutique Lady was Jane Carruthers, the wife of a prominent Memphis insurance executive and an active member of the Junior League, Memphis Country Club, and various local charity organizations. In the summer of 1977, Jane and Ewing Carruthers played tennis with friends Sue and Gene Greener, and then had them to their home for dinner. That evening, Sue Greener mentioned that her daughter Cindy's new husband, Jay Stein, planned to open a Memphis outlet for his quality discount store and she asked if Jane would be interested in working at the new store. College educated, Carruthers had worked as a stewardess with Chicago and Southern Airlines (which later merged with Delta), but had given up her career when she married twenty-five years earlier. Now that her four children were grown, the idea of working at the store sounded like fun, but she didn't think that possible since, with all of her civic and volunteer obligations, she could only work one day a week. Nevertheless, several weeks later, Sue Greener introduced Jane Carruthers to her son-in-law, and Jay hired her on the spot to work only on Wednesdays.

Carruthers started at the Memphis Stein Mart on Wednesday, September 15, one week after its grand opening. She enthusiastically told all of her friends about how much fun she was having and, perhaps more importantly, showed off the new clothes and accessories she had bought at the store, and bought at an employee discount. Within two months, she had interested three of her closest friends — Ann Stevens, Jan Bell, and Margaret Krausnick — to join Stein Mart as one-day-a-week salesladies. These four friends all belonged to the Memphis Country Club and various civic and social organizations; their husbands knew each other and their children went to the same schools. Now they became "the original four Boutique Ladies." Other socially prominent women would join Stein Mart in the months ahead, but these four always would be remembered as the first ones.

Neither Carruthers nor her colleagues had any retail experience, but followed Jay's advice to treat the customers just as they would if entertaining them in their own homes. Carl Davis, the store manager, thought this idea sounded crazy and questioned why women who didn't have to work would want to do that. His initial efforts to get these women placed on the payroll did little to alleviate his doubts. "I asked one of the ladies for her social security number," Davis recalls. "She looked at me strangely and said, 'I AM socially secure. I don't need a number!' Another one told me, ' I don't know what that is. You'll have to call my husband's secretary.'" Davis freely admits that he felt "somewhat intimidated" by his new employees.

Davis's reservations soon vanished as these part-time women began to attract to Stein Mart, through word-of-mouth testimonials in the social circles in which they traveled, an increasing number of affluent, fashion-conscious women with the financial means to spend large sums of money on clothing and accessories. Not only did these part-timers bring in lots of customers, but they also bought lots of merchandise themselves, taking advantage of their 25 percent discount (on already deeply discounted prices) and the "house account" that allowed them to charge their purchases. Davis even remembers getting some phone calls from irate husbands, who complained, "You call this a job? I'm paying out more than she's ever going to bring in!"

At first, these women worked on the sales floor in the women's department. But shortly after the store opened, Jay remembers Annette Lichterman, whose husband had helped the Steins locate the site, suggesting to him that he "reserve a corner of the store for treasures. . . . like a little boutique within the store." Similar suggestions came from Jane Carruthers and her friends. So Jay had the gift department moved to the center of the store, and designated the space in the front, on the right side, for a separate department with the more upscale women's fashions. He had a carpenter build a little fence around the area, to set it off from the rest of the store, and hired a painter to paint in script on the wall, "Le Boutique."

Several problems soon surfaced. For one, Jake Stein didn't like the new Boutique area. On his first trip to Memphis after it had been set up, Jake made disparaging comments about the little fence and threatened to have it torn down. When Emil Moos — quite cultured and fluent in several languages — visited the store, he observed that obviously no one spoke French, since proper grammar would require the feminine La Boutique. Soon afterwards, the painter returned to correct the mistake.

34. Emil Moos and Jay Stein at a store opening in the early 1990s.

The Boutique area also had no dressing rooms, so Carl Davis found some oriental screens with bamboo frames that had been for sale and he had them tied together to make two small enclosures. These makeshift dressing rooms proved flimsy and occasionally fell down while women were changing. And in the winter, with the Boutique area near one of the front doors, it could become quite uncomfortable to try on new clothes when the cold air blew into the store.

Despite these minor annoyances, the Boutique concept became an immediate hit with women customers. They liked having the higher-end, designer fashions concentrated in one area, and enjoyed the attentive personal service that they received from the Boutique Ladies. In reminiscing about their experiences at Stein Mart, the original four have lots of stories. On one occasion, when three of them were working at the same time, a woman came to the Boutique who had never shopped there before. She informed them that she normally bought all her clothing from the L. L. Bean catalogue, but needed something more fancy for a wedding. They triple-teamed this customer, helping her select a stylish skirt and blouse, but the store did not have any matching shoes. So Margaret Krausnick fitted her for a pair of dressy shoes, and then

35. Advertisement for "la Boutiques de Stein Mart."

took the shoes home and dyed them so that they matched the skirt. Now that's customer service!

La Boutique was loosely structured at the beginning, with the women working out their own schedules and trading hours, and even sometimes working in other departments as needed. After several years, a more formal structure evolved, with a group of twelve to fourteen regulars who worked

A SUCCESSFUL DAY IN THE BOUTIQUE

- Arrive at the store smiling between 9:40 and 9:45 am – you are beginning a great day as a boutique lady!
- Check newspaper for ad that day.
- Park away from the store to give the customer choice parking. As you go into the store, check the display windows.
- Check employee Bulletin Board.
- Wear your nametag on your upper right shoulder, where it is easily read by customers.
- It is store policy not to wear merchandise unless you have previously paid for it. We do, however, encourage you to try on (if the store is not busy or during your 15-minute break) any garment that you are curious about. This will help you be more informed about the merchandise we carry in our store.
- Check departments before the store opens – take note of any specials or new and exciting items that may have arrived. Familiarize yourself with all of the merchandise, especially in accessories, ladies and boutiques.
- Learn as much as possible about the merchandise such as fabric content, care and sizing. Share your knowledge with your co-workers, i.e. some manufacturers fit large, others small.
- Ask the department manager what the day's game plan is.
- Be enthusiastic and give personal attention to customers throughout the day. LISTEN TO THE CUSTOMER! If you must assist a customer in another department, please make sure your co-workers are aware and that the boutique is not left unattended.
- Keep dressing rooms clean, particularly after your own customers and remember take clothes back to other departments.
- Check all racks in the boutique
  - Make sure smaller sizes are up front.
  - Straighten hangers and garments
  - Turn hangers so that all go in one direction
  - Check to see if right styles are together. Check vendors.
  - Steam any new arrivals as they come into the Boutique during the day.
- If not busy with a customer, there is always something to do:
  - Fold sweaters, tidy clothes, and size them.
  - Call your friends to advise them of any new merchandise that has arrived.
- If you ever feel there is a security problem punch intercom and ask for security.
- Take damaged merchandise and customer complaints to the Service Desk or to the store manager.
- Ask customers to use the head covers when trying on clothes to protect the clothes from make-up stains.
- Be creative in wardrobe building; bring customers scarves, belts, and jewelry to help complete the look they want to achieve.
- Be alert! Ask each customer if she needs any help. Listen to her, Answer, and then help! Remember anyone can be a mystery shopper!
- We are given a 30-minute lunch with a mid-morning 15-minute break and a mid-afternoon 15-minute break. Please do your personal shopping during your lunch period or after your work day is complete.
- Smile, you have had another great day in the Boutique! Punch out on the time clock and have a grand evening!

36. 1994 guidelines for the Boutique Ladies, entitled "A Successful Day in the Boutique." When the Boutique Ladies program first started in Memphis, Jane Carruthers, as team leader, prepared a one-page, handwritten listing of instructions, which concluded with the admonition, "Please wear hose and do not chew gum." With the growth of the Boutique program and the establishment of a corporate coordinator in the Jacksonville headquarters, these guidelines became longer and more formalized. These January 1994 guidelines are five pages long. We have selected key bullet points to fit this single-page display.

37. & 38. On November 5, 1997, on the night before the grand opening of Store No. 149 (the fourth Stein Mart store in Memphis), Stein Mart celebrated twenty years in Memphis with a "Blues and Barbeque" event at the Rendezvous Restaurant. At this dinner, the four original Boutique Ladies received their twenty-year service pins. On the left, Jan Bell laughs as Jay recounts a story about how the store operated in 1977; on the right, Margaret Krausnick, Ann Stevens, and Jane Carruthers

one or two days a week. Jane Carruthers acted as group leader, and she maintained a list of substitutes (and their phone numbers) who could fill in when trips, or illnesses, or other obligations intervened. Each day, a minimum of two women would be scheduled for the Boutique area. Boutique Ladies were encouraged to look over all new merchandise and, if something "special" had arrived, to call friends or regular customers who might have an interest. If someone did but couldn't come to the store, the Boutique Ladies could take the clothes, and any matching accessories, out of the store for the evening and bring them to the person's house to let her try them on. The Boutique Ladies also tried to maintain a certain ambiance in their department, and when not waiting on customers would be straightening merchandise and making sure that the free coffee remained hot and fresh. During the Christmas shopping season, the Boutique Ladies worked extra hours at a special "men's night." An advertisement in the *Memphis Commercial-Appeal* promised, "Our resident experts will be on hand to offer their advice to all the men in Memphis looking for that special gift." The ad also promised refreshments, free gift-wrapping, and "informal modeling."

The "Boutique Ladies" concept became so successful that a waiting list had to be developed, and women would be placed on the substitute list for years waiting for a regular one-day-a-week opening. To be a Boutique Lady became an experience more than just a job. It was, in some respects, like joining a sorority. You weren't just an employee, but instead what the company considered a "Stein Mart ambassador to the community." And this special feeling was cultivated by Jay Stein — and also, once he became comfortable with the concept, by Jake, as well as Freda and later other company executives. Jay visited the Memphis store frequently, and he always sought out the Boutique Ladies, paying them extra attention and asking for their opinions on fashions and merchandise. The Boutique Ladies felt almost like part of the family. Thus, as Jay prepared to open more Stein Mart stores, adding new Boutique departments became an important part of the marketing strategy. The existing Boutique Ladies eagerly sought to help, calling friends in Nashville, Louisville, and other cities to recruit them as new Boutique Ladies. For years, the original four traveled to all new store openings, working at the grand openings and showing their new Boutique sisters how it was done. On one occasion, at the grand opening of the Jackson store, because of a mix-up, no women had been hired for the Boutique area. So Jane Carruthers and her three compatriots hired a full Boutique staff that first day from among women who came into the store to shop.

As Stein Mart added new stores, the number of Boutique Ladies grew, and the company even experimented briefly with a second "Sea Island Boutique" department, featuring classic, southern sportswear. By the twentieth anniversary of the hiring of the first four, Stein Mart had 2,600 Boutique Ladies. Prominent members of the Boutique sorority included the wife of the former governor of Tennessee and the wife of Baton Rouge's mayor. As their numbers grew, the company designated a full-time corporate coordinator. While the individual store manager had responsibility for ensuring that scheduling and payroll functions ran smoothly, beginning in the mid-1980s Jozette Read began working as the first liaison between the Boutique Ladies in the stores and the corporate headquarters staff, ensuring that these fashion-conscious women had access to company buyers so as to provide input and feedback concerning merchandise purchases. Read also became involved in establishing a more formal process for hiring Boutique Ladies as new stores opened. She initially screened recommendations from existing women, and then traveled to the new store locations to interview candidates and select the "Boutique leader." Read and the new leader then would select the rest of the Boutique staff. In 1988, Read's department began publishing a bimonthly newsletter, "Boutique High-Brow," with fashion updates, company announcements, and news about Boutique Ladies from throughout the company.

Stein Mart Store No. 2 in Memphis proved a huge success, and the "Boutique Ladies" concept played an important part in generating its strong sales performance. The Memphis store experimented with other ways to make the shopping experience more upscale and more enjoyable. In the early 1980s, for example, it added a French bread and pastry shop called "la baquette." Managed on a franchise basis by a downtown Memphis restaurant, "la baquette" — far different from the Stein Mart lunch counter at the Greenville store with its hot dogs, hamburgers, and more basic food selections — served gourmet lunches from 11 a.m. to 3 p.m. each day. This experiment only lasted approximately one year, and no initiatives ever achieved the level of success enjoyed by the La Boutique.

Looking back, Jay credits Carl Davis and Larry Shelton for their strong management and the effective way that they implemented new approaches to create a more upscale discount shopping environment. They did not receive a lot of day-to-day guidance from either Jay, who concentrated his energies on upgrading the merchandise and trying to establish more stable purchasing arrangements, or his father. Jake continued to focus his attention on the Greenville store during the week. On weekends, Jake and the whole family often made the two- to three-hour drive to Memphis to check on merchandise and visit with the staff. It was probably a good thing that Jake didn't take more interest, because he often failed to understand what kind of store Jay wanted to build. During those first years, merchandise would be shipped back and forth between the two stores, often with minimal record-keeping involved. Once when the Greenville store ran short on men's suits, Jake called and asked for a dozen suits until a new shipment arrived. "When I asked what price range of suits he wanted," Davis remembers, "Jake responded, 'It doesn't matter, but I won't sell anything over $100 down here.' If I sent him a $200 suit, he would mark it to $99 anyway. So I knew he wasn't on the same playing field with us." On another occasion, when Jay was away, Jake came to Memphis and decided to hold some "blue light" specials, hardly in keeping with his son's efforts to upgrade the store's image. Jake had brought a large pole with a flag on top, and he had Davis's son walk around the store with the pole and flag, stopping in different departments as Jake announced over the PA system that for the next ten or fifteen minutes certain items would be 50 percent off. When Jake tried to send the boy with the flag into the Boutique, Jane Carruthers physically blocked the entrance.

While Jake might not fully have comprehended what Jay wanted to do, he could not help but notice that, whatever it was, the Memphis store sold lots of merchandise. Stein Mart did not have many performance measurement tools at the time, and its financial controls remained primitive. After the store's fiscal year ended on January 31 each year, Jake would take his bank account records to Bill Tarver's accounting firm, which then would complete, with no audit or review performed, a balance sheet and operating statement. For the fiscal year ending January 31, 1977, Stein Mart's single Greenville store reported sales of $3.3 million and an after-tax profit of $85,910. Two years later, as of January 31, 1979 — the first fiscal year that included a full year of the Memphis operation — sales had increased to $8 million and net profits to $320,741. Although the operating statement contained no breakdown of results between the two stores, even Jake could figure out that expanding into Memphis had been the right thing to do.

The success of Memphis proved especially gratifying to Jay — "I will always have a very soft spot for Memphis. Greenville laid the foundation, but Memphis brought us to the table." With the Memphis store having exceeded all expectations, it became the prototype for future stores. More expansion was on the way.

39. *"We're going to Spoil you!" advertisement from 1985.*

CHAPTER 4

Building a Greater Dream

"It was always my father's retail philosophy . . . to have a unique niche in the marketplace. Meaning, do something different. He still does in Greenville, catering to the merchant needs of that community. . . . But, as is typical of most sons of achieving fathers, I wanted to do something, too. On my own. We wanted very strongly to remain in the discount business, but I wanted to do it on a different taste level. A taste level that I can relate to."

– Jay Stein, as quoted in *The Florida Times-Union*
"Jay Stein Pins Hopes on New Home," November 13, 1984

*I*n October 1979, Stein Mart opened Store No. 3 in Nashville, Tennessee, and soon afterwards began planning to open yet another in Louisville, Kentucky. With the success experienced at each new store, Jay Stein proved to his father the wisdom — and the profitability — of his plans for taking the company in new directions. Thus, Jay began to pursue in earnest his vision of "building a greater dream," one built on the foundations established by his grandfather and father, but which had a new focus on merchandise quality and a search for new customers far beyond those found in Greenville, Mississippi.

As the number of stores increased so did the need for better operational procedures to manage a multi-location company. Slowly, rudimentary controls started to be put in place. In Memphis, Carl Davis implemented some of the basics that he had learned at Shainberg's — using so-called "green sheets" to log-in new merchandise and check it against invoices; establishing procedures for recording cash register overages and shortages, and tying cash register balances to bank deposits; starting to track markdowns and price changes; and putting in place other procedures that by the late 1970s were long overdue. Davis considered some practices to be just plain "scary." When the Steins came to Memphis, Jake often invited him to go to lunch, and then "he would open the register and get a handful of money;" or Freda would see some clothes that she liked and ask the clerk to box it and put it in her car. Davis finally had to tell them that he realized they owned the store and could do whatever they wanted, but there needed to be some basic record-keeping. "I told Mr. Stein, 'You want money out of the register, just tell me how much. I'll get it out and leave a note to record it.'"

Back in Greenville, the company's new controller also attempted to set up some controls. Born and raised in Greenville, Clayton Roberson had returned home after graduating from Mississippi State and joined the CPA firm of Tarver, Tarver, Kirby & Bradley. One of his assignments with the firm had been to prepare the annual tax returns for Stein Mart and the United Dollar Store. In the summer of 1977, Jay approached Bill Tarver to ask if he could talk with Roberson about working for Stein Mart, and in October of that year — one month after the Memphis store opened — Roberson joined Stein Mart with responsibilities for the accounting functions at both stores.

Stein Mart had no formal organizational chart and Roberson worked for both Jay and Jake as a one-person accounting department, with some informal assistance from Stanley Sherman. Not until mid-1979 did the volume increase to the point where he could hire an accounts payable clerk. One of the biggest challenges Roberson faced involved convincing Jake that the company needed to conduct a physical inventory of the store, without which any financial operating numbers would be suspect. A formal inventory had never been performed in the company's history. Roberson recalls, "Mr. Stein, being a merchant and not an accountant and a control person, did not understand all of the time and effort devoted to getting that store in Greenville ready to take a physical inventory and then having someone come in and count every single piece of merchandise in that store to determine what the inventory valuation should be." Roberson finally convinced Jake and then contracted with an outside company to conduct that first inventory.

Jay realized that if the company continued opening new stores, it would need more management talent. In late 1979, not long after the Nashville store opened, Jay talked with Emil Moos about wanting to hire an experienced manager. Moos agreed, and helped to persuade Jake that it was a good idea. Moos gave Jay the name of a prominent executive search firm that Saks used. Jay did not know exactly what to look for, but he knew that he needed "someone that had the experience I didn't, that had run bigger businesses than I had run, and someone who had a conservative business posture that would complement my aggressive posture." He interviewed three or four people, but couldn't get comfortable with any of the candidates. Then the headhunter, who had previously worked for Genesco, suggested that a senior executive from that company, Jack Williams, might be interested.

John Hayden Williams Jr. had been born and raised in Nashville, where his father worked for the Baptist Sunday School Board, and later the Executive Committee of the Southern Baptist Convention. He attended Belmont College in Nashville and during his senior year married his high school sweetheart, Norma. Jack had dual majors in business and psychology, with a minor in economics, and began his career in retailing by accident. His freshman year, he started working a part-time night job for Genesco, operating the punch-card IBM equipment used in the 1950s. When Genesco acquired its first computer, Jack trained to be one of the company's first console computer operators. After graduating from college in 1959, Genesco offered him a position in its management training program, and Jack spent the next year working in a shoe factory, selling shoes in a retail store, and traveling with a shoe salesman selling wholesale accounts.

Genesco had its origins in the 1920s as the General Shoe Corporation, but in the mid-1950s it signed a consent degree with the Justice Department that limited future acquisitions in the shoe business. Consequently, Genesco began to diversify. It purchased two companies that manufactured men's clothing, several men's specialty clothing store chains, the holding company that owned department stores Tiffany's and Bonwit Teller, and the S. H. Kress variety stores. During the next twenty years, Jack had numerous assignments with Genesco and its many subsidiaries, including data processing manager at the Chicago offices of the Formfit Company that manufactured bras and girdles; general merchandise manager and then president of S. H. Kress's Birmingham-based Elmore's division; corporate staff jobs at Genesco's Nashville headquarters in human resources and several troubleshooter assignments; and finally, early in 1980, appointment as president of S. H. Kress.

In the late 1970s, Jack spent several years commuting between Nashville and New York City. At the time, Genesco had decided to close two of its money-losing retail operations, the Whitehouse & Hardy men's clothing chain and Bonwit Teller. It was during that time that Jay and Jack met for the first time. In mid-1979, Jay needed fixtures for the new Nashville store, and Jack had fixtures for sale from Bonwit Teller's flagship store on Fifth Avenue. Jay and Cindy were in New York, and they met Jack at Bonwit Teller where they negotiated the price. Jack enjoys telling how "Cindy later said that she thought I was the meanest thing on two feet."

These fixtures negotiations evidently had not left any bad impression with Jay, and Jack thinks it may have been a positive since Jay, himself "a wonderful negotiator," would have appreciated good, tough negotiating. The headhunter arranged for Jay and Jack to meet several times, and then Jay asked Jack to interview with Emil Moos. Having passed that test, Jack flew to Greenville to meet Jake Stein. Jack found the prospects of working at Stein Mart intriguing. Even though he had only recently been named president of S. H. Kress, he had grown tired the past several years of closing stores and supervising a general pull-back in operations, and he feared that more of the same lay ahead with S. H. Kress. The opportunity to join a growing and expanding business seemed more exciting, and Jay's enthusiasm and vision of where Stein Mart could go energized him. Jack Williams agreed to join Stein Mart as executive vice president, effective July 1, 1980.

Jay Stein's hiring of Jack Williams represented perhaps the most critical decision impacting whether or not Stein Mart would be able to transform itself into a national retail organization. Two decades later, every key executive with the company agrees that the two of them made a perfect match, and that their talents and strengths complemented each other — Jay, the visionary builder, with a flair for fashion and extraordinary merchandising instincts; and Jack, the experienced operations man, with a calm, measured management approach and a conservative financial orientation.

Jack Williams recognized from the first that working for a small, family-owned business represented a new set of challenges. From day one, Jack told his new boss that he would not be a "yes man," that he would tell Jay exactly what he thought and why he thought it. He did understand "that the sign out front says 'Stein'," and if they disagreed, and Jack couldn't convince Jay, he would do it Jay's way. The only exception would be if their disagreement involved what Jack considered "a matter of integrity," in which case, if he couldn't win Jay to his side, he would resign. But that never happened, and serious disagreements occurred infrequently and always resolved amicably.

Jay and Jack have very different personalities and management styles. Jay has been described as "passionate" about retailing, an energetic, impulsive entrepreneur; Jack is seen as more reserved and more deliberate, a cost-conscious "numbers guy." Nevertheless, Jay is quick to admit that the company could not have succeeded without Jack Williams. "Jack was my right and my left hand.... I certainly deferred to him all of the time on organizational issues and operational issues. Jack was very smart, very methodical.... Only rarely did we have a disagreement. It would be when Jack would be more conservative in personnel than I would wish to be. I would want to hire for this and this and this, and he would say we can't afford but this." They also sometimes took a different approach to evaluating personnel or new initiatives. Jay recalls, "I was always quicker than Jack to decide if it worked or not. Jack would always say let's give it another month or two. And sometimes he was right, and sometimes I was right." Over the years, the two men grew close, both professionally and personally. As Jack once explained to a newspaper reporter, "Neither one of us ever had a brother. And we've almost gotten to the point where it's a family relationship between the two of us."[1]

This successful management partnership between Jay Stein and Jack Williams still lay in the not-too-distant future as Jack started his Stein Mart career in July 1980. He found a company with little infrastructure and limited staff, with weak financial controls and a focus on short-term activities as opposed to long-term planning. The immediate task focused on getting ready for Store No. 4 in Louisville, purchasing merchandise and finding managers and staff with the opening less than three months away. With the Louisville store successfully opened, Jack soon discovered that there were simply too few people to do too many things, and that at the ownership/management level, everyone was expected to do a little bit of everything. Lines of responsibility remained vague. The company had no full-time buyers, and, in general, Jay bought all of the women's clothing (with assistance from Phil Dobuler, on retainer to look for good opportunities among his New York contacts), Jake bought fabrics and linens, and Freda and Cindy bought gifts. Jack took over buying responsibilities for men's clothing, in addition to his administrative and finance duties. Every six to eight weeks, all of them would "go to market" in New York City, with the stores left to get along on their own. After the opening of Store No. 5 in Little Rock, Arkansas, Carl Davis assumed responsibility for traveling among the stores to supervise operational issues, with Larry Shelton given management responsibility for the Memphis store, although he too found himself subject to being drafted for "doing other things."

Jay hoped to open at least two new stores each year, even though his father remained skeptical. Nevertheless, Jake acquiesced, in part because each newly opened store had proven successful and in part because several friends and business confidantes — Emil Moos and the family's (as well as the company's) attorney, Frank Hunger — encouraged him to support Jay's expansion efforts. The process for selecting store locations, however, was not very sophisticated, with target cities drawn from a ranking of cities published in a national trade magazine, *Chain Store Age Executive*. From those southeastern cities listed, if Jack could negotiate a lease in an attractive location, that became the next expansion site. In 1982, Stein Mart opened Store No. 6 in Jackson, Mississippi, and no. 7 in Mobile, Alabama; the next year, no. 8 in Jacksonville, Florida and no. 9 in New Orleans. This expansion schedule presented challenges in terms of mobilizing the manpower necessary to open new stores, finding management talent to run them, and developing a more sophisticated financial framework to better control this expanding network of stores.

New store openings became big events and energized everyone among Stein Mart's key managers. Several weeks before the scheduled opening, Jay, Jack, Carl Davis, and their wives would go to the new city to hire staff, arrange fixtures, put up signs, price and display merchandise, and handle the countless last-minute details. Jack remembers how he and Davis would work in the warehouse in jeans and tee shirts, shoulder-to-shoulder with teenagers hired as temporary help, unloading merchandise, flattening the empty cardboard boxes, and then hauling the packing materials to the dumpster. When opening day arrived, the teenagers would be shocked when Jack showed up in a coat and tie and turned out to be one of the bosses. On one occasion, during Stein Mart's first expansion outside of the South — to Denver, Colorado — Davis overheard two young part-timers working in the stockroom. One asked, "Who are all these people with Southern accents?" and the other responded, "I'm not sure who they are, but the way I've got this thing figured is if they ask you to do something, you probably ought to do it."

As opening day grew closer, Jake and Freda would come, as would a number of their Greenville friends. The original four Boutique Ladies

40. Advertisement announcing that Stein Mart "has come to Little Rock," with the grand opening scheduled for March 17, 1981.

— Jane Carruthers, Ann Stevens, Jan Bell, and Margaret Krausnick — would show up to help get the Boutique area off to a good start. The openings became a time for fun and socializing amidst a lot of hard work. The night before the opening, Jay would host a big dinner, and the original Boutique Ladies often entertained with songs and skits. On opening day, generally a Wednesday or Thursday, there would be an in-store luncheon for all employees as a reward for getting everything ready. All the Stein Mart executives and their wives worked, helping to wait on the crowds of customers attracted by advertisements promising great bargains. It was not unusual to see Jake, or Emil Moos, or Frank Hunger, or some other family friend bagging merchandise at the checkout counters. Jack Williams remembers at the Little Rock opening that the checkout lines grew so long that Moos volunteered to operate a temporary cash register station. Jack chuckles as he recalls the slow-moving line as the near-sighted Moos struggled to read the price tags and fumbled with the register — but at the end of the day, Moos beamed with pride when his register balanced with only a ten- cent variance. On the Sunday after the opening, the store would run a full-page advertisement in the local newspaper, with a simple message, just changing the name to suit the city — "Thank You, Little Rock! We Love You Too!" — and photos of a full parking lot and a packed store. Afterwards, Carl Davis would get the first dollar that came into the register and have it framed and hung in the manager's office. While store openings in these first years were "grand" and a great time was had by all, they proved time-consuming and distracted management attention from existing stores. The problems that could arise became more evident when the pace of openings increased beyond one or two per year.

Finding qualified store managers was one problem that Jay and Jack solved relatively easily. Before the Louisville store opened, they had interviewed a number of candidates to manage the store, but it turned into a painful process and neither had confidence that they had selected well. With more store openings on the horizon, they decided that a program should be established so that potential managers could be trained in existing stores. At the time, Carl Davis ran the Memphis store with Larry Shelton as his assistant, and now a second assistant, Jon Rogers, joined management, with the announced intention that Rogers would become manager of the next store to be opened. The following

41. *Advertisement thanking Little Rock, Arkansas, for the successful opening of Stein Mart Store No. 5.*

year, Rogers was named manager of Store No. 5 in Little Rock. From that point, the organizational structure for all stores changed to allow for two assistant managers, thus building an ever-larger talent pool of potential managers who had been trained in the Stein Mart way of do-ing business. This approach for ensuring qualified internal candidates for future store manager openings remains in effect today.

Jack formalized Stein Mart's banking relationships. Initially, as each store opened, it set up its own separate checking account. Store managers wrote checks from these accounts to pay for everything from merchandise shipments to incidental expenses. To get a better control on expense management, Jack had these accounts closed and instead set up a single consolidated account. Although Jake and Jay both served on bank boards, the company did not have any formal credit agreements. Jack put the company's banking business out for bid and solicited sev-eral regional banks for a formal line of credit. Deposit Guaranty Bank, based in Jackson, won the competitive bidding and gave Stein Mart its first line of credit for $4 million, together with a cash management account. Nevertheless, Jake never did understand the need for these new financial arrangements, and he remained especially adverse to debt. Once when Jay and his wife were vacationing in Europe, the company had to draw approximately $1 million under its line of credit to pay for the purchase of its fall merchandise. Jake had to sign the note, and Jack recalls, "Jay's father was none too pleased."

As part of the process of seeking a bank credit facility, Jack and Jay prepared a formal financial presentation in the fall of 1981. The pre-sentation included some historical financial data, as well as pro forma projections that sales would more than triple in the next three years and net earnings quadruple based upon current plans "to expand selectively at a rate of two stores per year." This presentation provides insights to the company strategy at the very beginning of its expansion program, at a time when it only had five stores.[2] Defining itself as "a discount fashion retailer, offering to its customer better current fashion merchandise at significant savings," the presentation emphasized Stein Mart positioning itself to take advantage of trends in retail merchandising that indicated "a continuing growth of consumer interest in better quality, brands, and ego satisfying merchandise." Stein Mart had developed "a fairly unique set of relationships...[with] some of the best fashion houses and makers of fine goods." Consequently, "Stein Mart's USP (unique selling proposition) continues to be both viable and very effective. Most discounters battle each other to see who can sell low-end goods at the cheapest price. Stein Mart has chosen a different approach, that of making better goods accessible to a broader market by discounting the prices. This approach is further unique in that the presentation of a broad selection of merchandise, at a consistently high taste level, is presented with the service and ambiance usually more associated with department stores and fine specialty stores than discounters." Twenty years, and some 260 stores later, this summary of what makes Stein Mart unique, and successful, still holds true.

✳ ✳ ✳ ✳ ✳

A year after the Memphis store opened, Jay Stein became president and chief executive officer of Stein Mart, Inc. While recognizing that his son needed to be given the authority to run the company, Jake (now in the position of chairman) remained a vocal adviser. Titles don't mean much in a family-owned business, and Jake continued to challenge Jay's ideas and to raise objections every time a new store expansion opportunity arose. Jake simply did not understand what his son hoped to accomplish. In September 1983, as everyone gathered in New Orleans to prepare for the opening of Store No. 9, Jack Williams remembers a conversation that he had with Jake. "Mr. Stein came to get me and said, 'Mr. Jack, I want you to have a cup of coffee with me.' We walked across the parking lot, and he put his arm around my shoulders and said, 'What the hell are you boys trying to do?' I looked at him and said, 'What do you mean?' He replied, 'Opening all these stores.' We had opened two that fall season. 'You all got enough now that you and Jay can have any kind of life you want to have and do whatever you want to do. You're going to kill yourselves opening all these stores.'"

Unbeknownst to Jake, an even more unsettling change was then under discussion — moving Stein Mart's headquarters out of Greenville. By September 1983, the company's key managers resided in three different cities — Jay, his parents, and Clayton Roberson and his accounting staff (now increased to eight) in Greenville; Jack and several advertising and merchandising assistants in Nashville; and Carl Davis and Larry Shelton in Memphis. It had become a cumbersome arrangement, with Jack periodically flying to Greenville and he and Jay meeting in Memphis a couple times each month. Jay estimated that he spent approximately 60 percent of his time traveling, either visiting the stores or buying merchandise.

By mid-1983, Jay and Jack talked often about the need to consolidate the company's senior staff members at a single location. Not only did that make sense from a management standpoint, but also from a company growth perspective. If Stein Mart planned to continue expanding its network of stores throughout the Southeast, and beyond, it would need to attract more management talent. It would be difficult to do so if the company continued to be based in Greenville. The local economy in Greenville remained in decline, air transportation into and out of the city was still inadequate, and the city did not have the educational and cultural institutions to make it attractive to relocating executives.

In considering possible alternatives, Nashville emerged as the leading candidate. Not only did Jack Williams already live there, but a number of local businessmen — including the owner of Nashville-based Service Merchandise, who had developed a strong friendship with Jay — had been lobbying them to choose their city. Jay came close to a decision that summer, but decided to wait until after the opening of the Jacksonville and New Orleans stores, both scheduled for September 1983. In the weeks before the Jacksonville opening, Jay and Jack and their wives stayed at the Ponte Vedra Club, located on the beaches of the Atlantic Ocean. As the four of them drove back and forth each day from their beachfront hotel to the University Boulevard store, and as they enjoyed the restaurants and walks on the beach, Jay decided that this might be the lifestyle he wanted. Jay had some unpleasant memories of Jacksonville from his prep school days twenty years earlier, but Jacksonville had changed. When he first suggested to Jack that perhaps they should reconsider where to move the company, Jack showed little enthusiasm since all of his family lived in Nashville. They asked Emil Moos for his opinion, and he said moving to Jacksonville would be "insane." But Jay kept insisting that Jacksonville might be the better choice, and over the next several months he and Jack made lists of the pros and cons. The biggest drawback for Jacksonville was its location, far to the east of the other stores grouped together in Mississippi, Tennessee, Kentucky, Arkansas, and Alabama. On the plus side, Florida would be a good place to recruit management. And unlike Nashville,

42. Jay Stein at the Jacksonville store on University Boulevard, 1984.

where Stein Mart would be just another company headquartered there, in Jacksonville Jay believed that Stein Mart "could make a difference in the community." So after considerable deliberation, Jay and Jack agreed on Jacksonville.

From a personal perspective, the decision to relocate had been difficult for Jay. Like his grandfather and father before him, he had established strong roots in the Greenville community. Except for his years at prep school and college, Jay had lived his entire life in Greenville, and now he would be leaving family and friends behind. Shortly after relocating to Jacksonville, Jay told a local newspaper reporter that the move "was a tremendous emotional step for me, having left where my family had lived for almost a century."[3] But from a business perspective, it was the right decision.

Once the decision had been made, Jay faced the difficult task of telling his parents. His father took the news well. Jake had grown weary of their frequent squabbling — as had Jay — and he became reconciled to being left alone to run the Greenville store the way he wanted, while Jay pursued a strategy that, while he didn't fully understand it, had been very successful. Jay's mother was more emotional. Freda took the news hard, unhappy that her son and his family would be moving from Greenville, especially as it had been less than a year since her first granddaughter had been born.

In early 1984, Stein Mart issued a press release officially announcing its move to Jacksonville, a decision based on the "belief that the city is a dynamic community poised for an explosive growth period over the next few years. Other attractive considerations were the quality of life Jacksonville offers and the warm acceptance extended by the community when Stein Mart opened a new store in the area." While Jacksonville's business community and Chamber of Commerce enthusiastically welcomed the decision, the response in Greenville was muted, even though Jay had told the *Delta Democrat-Times* only two years earlier that "we don't intend to consolidate our operations elsewhere." The reaction of the Greenville community surprised Jay — "They didn't think they were losing much. I had a call from one person from the Chamber asking 'How many people are you taking with you?' He didn't say, 'How can we keep you here?'...I said we were taking three or four. They didn't do a lot to keep us from leaving." So in July 1984, fourteen Stein Mart associates and their families moved to Jacksonville, and the company

43. *Jay's family hosted a 40th birthday party at his Jacksonville home in 1985. From the left, Jay, Joe Stein Jr., Frank Hunger, and family friend Martin Uhlfelder.*

44. Jay at home with his two daughters, two-year-old Berry and five-year-old Jay Meredith, spring 1988.

set up its first consolidated headquarters in leased office space in the Deerwood area on the city's Southside.

After relocating its company headquarters to Jacksonville, Stein Mart spent the rest of the 1980s and early 1990s modernizing its operations. It escalated the pace of store openings, developed a more structured corporate organization, and refined its merchandising strategies. In mid-1984, Stein Mart had eleven stores, all in the Southeast, and reported $48.3 million in sales for its last fiscal year. By the end of 1991, its network of stores had grown to forty-five, still concentrated in the Southeast but also in Texas, Oklahoma, and Colorado, with sales of $278.3 million.

During this 1984 to 1991 period, the number of store openings accelerated from two per year to six or seven per year. With this more aggressive expansion schedule, plus the ever-increasing network of stores that needed to be managed, procedures for conducting the store-opening process required more structure. The old "family reunion" approach, where Stein Mart's senior managers dropped everything to spend several weeks — along with their wives and other key associates — preparing for the grand opening, had become impractical. No one remained back at headquarters to manage the company, a problem that became especially acute in August and September 1985 when three new stores all opened within two months. With company executives distracted by these openings, in the words of Carl Davis "enough went to hell back home" that it became obvious a new approach to opening and managing the stores would be needed.

Up to that point, Jack Williams had kept responsibility for supervising store operations. He relied primarily on Carl Davis to visit the different stores and to assist store managers. Now, Jack moved to implement a more formal structure. During the past several years, Davis had assumed, often by default, a lot of back-room functions, such as providing logistical support for the new headquarters building and coordinating administrative services relating to purchasing fixtures and signs, negotiating contracts for maintenance services, and other non-merchandising activities. Jack asked Davis to direct his efforts full-time to these administrative functions, and selected Roy Roberts, manager of the Nashville store, to transfer to Jacksonville to supervise store operations. During the next several years, as the number of stores increased, Jack selected other experienced store managers — Bob Brooks, Max Stanford, and Lester "Lee" Blake — to join Roberts as regional directors of stores. Each had responsibility for about a dozen stores, working closely with the managers on staffing, customer service, and presentation of merchandise.

With this new regional organizational structure, store opening responsibilities shifted more to the regional directors. While Carl Davis still had responsibility for negotiating with vendors for fixtures and signs, arranging for utility hook-ups, and ensuring that all of those necessary behind-the-scenes tasks got completed on time, the regional directors organized task forces from the existing stores in their regions. They asked different department managers and experienced salespeople, on a rotating basis, to help with stocking the new store, training the new staff, and assisting with the first few days of operation. This new approach had several advantages, one being that it provided a so-called "cross-pollination" in the company as it allowed employees and managers from different stores the opportunity to meet other Stein Mart associates, and also it promoted a more standardized approach to operating issues. Selection to one of these task forces came to be considered by

45. Jack Williams.

employees as a reward and recognition for a job well done. Only on the day of the actual opening did Jay, Jack, and other corporate executives attend, spending just the one day meeting with new employees and greeting customers.

While Jack began to build a team of regional directors to help manage the expanding network of stores, he also addressed how to best handle his other operational responsibilities, which included finance, human resources, technology, real estate, and all other non-merchandising activities. Jack, known for being very frugal in how he spent the company's money, tried to balance the need for more management infrastructure with concerns for controlling expenses. In the information technology area, Jack — working in close coordination with the merchandising side of the company — oversaw substantial investments in software applications and computer hardware needed to improve tracking sales and monitoring inventory. But the data processing area proved somewhat frustrating, especially for someone focused on expense control, as technology constantly changed and the expected benefits promised by both outside vendors and in-house data processing staff oftentimes proved slow to materialize. Consequently, Jack went through three different information systems managers during this period.

In contrast, Jack tried to keep expenses to a minimum in the real estate area. The first few store openings had proven so successful that he and Jay decided that future site selections should follow the same pattern — stores with approximately 38,000 square feet located in strip shopping centers, with lots of parking and with co-tenants that might appeal to a similar customer base. The company would avoid locations in shopping malls, and it would only lease facilities, not buy property — the only store that did not fit that requirement was the Greenville Stein Mart, owned by a Stein family partnership. Jack did not hire anyone to help him with real estate, insisting on personally visiting all potential store sites and negotiating all store leases.

One of Jack's principal concerns involved improving financial controls. Having determined that the compilation financial statements prepared by Greenville's Tarver CPA firm, with no audit or review, did not give management sufficiently detailed operating information, Jack hired Price Waterhouse to perform auditing services for the company. Beginning with the January 31, 1984, fiscal year-end, Price Waterhouse prepared in-depth, audited financial statements, and during the first several years also provided the company with detailed recommendations for improving internal accounting controls and administrative procedures. These recommendations ranged from establishing new general ledger cost centers and strengthening the purchasing control system to developing an accounting procedures manual and drafting a formal business plan. Working closely with the company's controller, Clayton Roberson, Jack pushed for improvements in these areas.

The early management structure remained quite simple. As Jay describes it, "Jack would take care of the operations and finances of the business, and I would do the merchandise until it got large enough that we felt we needed expertise beyond our own. And it happened to me first." The opening of new stores led to the need for the purchase of increased volumes of merchandise and the distribution of that merchandise to more separate points of sales. Jay realized that he could not devote so much of his time and energy to the merchandising function, as other management issues demanded his attention. As the complexity of the merchandising activities grew, Stein Mart would not only need to organize a merchandising system, but also would benefit by acquiring some expertise from professional merchants who had worked for other retail organizations.

Several months before the headquarters move to Jacksonville, Jay hired Bill Howell as Stein Mart's first general merchandise manager (GMM). Initally, Howell worked out of the Nashville store, where Jack Williams had his office, and then he and a staff of a half dozen buyers that he had hired moved to Jacksonville. Being the GMM for an organization in which the president has a flair for fashion and strong ideas about what kind of merchandise to promote would be a difficult assignment for anyone. As Jack commented after observing the dynamics of the situation, "Jay wanted somebody he could share merchandising responsibility with, but he wasn't going to share too much. He was still going to be heavily involved with the merchandising decisions of the company." So it proved to be a tough transition for both Jay and Bill Howell, but especially so for Howell, who never before had been a GMM. Not surprising, neither Howell nor his immediate successor, Emil Wulfe, enjoyed a long tenure as GMM. After Wulfe left the company, Jay hired a New York executive search firm to identify possible replacements. One of the candidates they found was Dwight Mason Allen, destined to be a key figure in Stein Mart's successes over the next decade.

Mason Allen had been born in Cucumber, West Virginia, where his father worked as an engineer in the coal mines. Because of his mother's health problems, the family needed to move to a better climate, relocating to Clearwater, Florida in 1950 when Allen was seven. Allen attended the University of Florida, where he majored in business. He had no intention of getting into retailing, but after graduation he worked part-time at Maas Brothers while waiting to attend basic training for the Army Reserve. When he returned from his six-month active duty training commitment, Allen had trouble finding a permanent job and agreed to join Maas Brothers' management training program, initially expecting to stay only for a year or two until he found something better. Part of Allied Stores, a major national department store chain, Tampa-based Maas Brothers benefited from Florida's tremendous population growth of the 1960s and 1970s, and the consequent booming retail business. Maas Brothers was growing, and Allen advanced rapidly. After three years, he had been promoted to a position as buyer in charge of purchasing ladies' sportswear for all Maas Brothers stores in Florida. During this time, Allen befriended the executive in charge of computer systems for the company. Allen agreed to have his area act as a "guinea pig" to test new ideas, and he became very computer literate, eventually serving on Maas Brothers' review board for company technology initiatives.

This computer orientation served Allen well when the May Company, another national retail chain with headquarters in St. Louis, sought to upgrade its technology capabilities in the early 1970s. Because he understood both merchandising and computer systems — a unique combination of skills at the time — Allen accepted a senior corporate staff job with the May Company, and he subsequently managed a number of special assignments that integrated technology with planning, research, and product development at all twelve of May's department store divisions. Even though Allen enjoyed the creative challenges of these corporate staff assignments, he wanted to get back on the operating side of the business and when he got the chance, he transferred to a divisional manager position with May's affiliate in Akron, Ohio. But Allen wanted to return to Florida, so in 1976 he joined J. B. Ivey & Company as the number two person in its Florida division, based in Winter Park. Allen enjoyed his time with Ivey's until the early 1980s when Marshall Field bought the company, and then Marshall Field shortly afterwards was acquired by British American Tobacco Industries (BATUS). Allen recalls, "I came to Ivey's to get into small-world retailing where you could be 'hands-on' and not have the big corporate world and now, all of a sudden, we have people from London trying to run the business." Ivey's had twelve stores in Florida and fourteen in North Carolina — with separate corporate offices in Winter Park and Charlotte — and they had been run as separate divisions, with very different mixes of merchandise given the different lifestyles in Florida and North Carolina. BATUS decided to combine the two divisions, despite the objections of Allen and other Ivey's executives.

At this juncture, at a time when Allen had begun to look for a new opportunity, the executive search firm contacted him about the Stein Mart position. He talked with Jay Stein, and continued discussions with Jay and Jack Williams for the next several months. Allen had some additional insights into the Stein Mart organization since Bill Howell, who had been the company's GMM several years earlier, now worked for him at Ivey's. In Allen's assessment, Stein Mart, like all entrepreneurial companies, could operate successfully until it reached a certain size and "then you hit an organizational plateau where you have to make some very serious future long-range decisions of where you're going, how you're going to get there, and what are the components of getting there. Jay and Jack were wise enough to see the plateau and realize that they were approaching that." Intrigued by Stein Mart and the opportunity to get back to "hands-on" retailing, Allen accepted the position of senior vice president and general merchandise manger, with responsibility for all merchandising and advertising.

Mason Allen brought a unique set of experiences to Stein Mart, especially his abilities to integrate technology with merchandising and his forward-looking emphasis on planning. Perhaps just as important, he had the interpersonal skills to develop good working relationships with both Jay and Jack and to become a valuable third member of the executive management team. Jay took an immediate liking to Allen, whose style and personality "fit the family." Allen recognized that Jay had "a fabulous fashion sense," and he worked to keep him fully engaged in issues regarding fashion, style, and merchandise presentation.

When Allen joined the company in 1986, a good portion of its merchandise still came from so-called "opportunity buys." That approach, however, made it difficult to manage inventory levels at a growing number of stores. Often stores would be left with too much of one product and too little of another. The customer that Stein Mart hoped to attract was the customer who normally shopped in department stores. This customer expected to find certain items always in stock when he or she visited the store, such as men's dress shirts, socks, and underwear. How to ensure a guaranteed assortment of this basic merchandise became one of Allen's first challenges as GMM. This required working with vendors on more forward advance buying of clothing that the company knew it would need, thus ensuring that various sizes and assortments of colors of basic merchandise — for example, men's dress shirts in white and blue — would always be in stock, at a good price, 365 days a year. So if a customer went to a Stein Mart store, in every department certain basic items would always be available, and these would then be supplemented by the opportunity buys.

Allen saw the need for more sales and inventory planning, and used his systems background to begin developing the analytical tools necessary to evaluate sales performance in different inventory categories on a store-by-store basis. Recognizing that there might be unique sales opportunities at different stores, the company sought to customize its inventory by location, with a Stein Mart store located near the beach in Florida, for example, having more swimsuits than dress shirts. The merchandising division began planning six months in advance for detailed inventory levels for each department, in each retail location. Systems that tracked sales performance against anticipated buys on a weekly and monthly basis allowed for the fine-tuning of merchandise levels.

All of these advances in sales and inventory management would only be possible with the establishment of a more professional staff of merchandise buyers. When Allen joined Stein Mart in 1986, the company only had about a dozen buyers to support its nearly twenty stores. The number of buyers doubled during the next five or six years, and then jumped dramatically as the rate of store openings accelerated in the early 1990s. By then, Allen had been elevated to senior executive vice president and chief merchandising officer, and had developed a more formal organizational structure with general and divisional merchandise managers responsible for supervising groups of buyers who had expertise in men's clothing, or ladies' sportswear, or other merchandising specialties. Allen remembers that by the mid-1990s, the company's merchandising division had four general

WHEN YOU CAN'T AFFORD LESS THAN THE BEST...STEIN MART. Designer fashion for men, women and children. Exquisite linens. Unique gifts and home decor. All the best for the holidays! With prices to match. 25% to 60% less than in other fine stores...every day!

Stein Mart
THE LOOK·THE NAME·THE PRICE

AUSTIN: NORTHWOOD PLAZA • 2900 W. ANDERSON LANE
SAN ANTONIO: CROSSROADS MALL • LINCOLN HEIGHTS SHOPPING CENTER

46. & 47. Advertisements from the 1980s.

merchandise managers, ten to twelve divisional managers, and forty buyers, each with one or two administrative assistants, for a total of more than 120 people. This expansion of Stein Mart's merchandising staff coincided with the difficult times experienced by a number of department stores in the late 1980s and early 1990s, problems caused not only by recessionary economic times but also because of mergers and leveraged buyouts among major retailers. As a result, a good market developed in which to recruit professional, experienced buyers who had worked for other major retailers, and Stein Mart offered attractive financial packages and the opportunity for advancement in a growing company.

In addition to developing better management systems and hiring more experienced buyers, Allen also worked to reshape the company's marketing approach. In Greenville and during the first wave of store expansions, newspaper advertisements focused on special bargain prices for specific items of merchandise and emphasized that this discounted

merchandise came from Saks, or Neiman-Marcus, or some other prominent, big-city department store. The advertisements were not very sophisticated, and Carl Davis remembers that during those first years in Memphis, Jake Stein would visit the store on the weekends and draw the ads for the next week on the white Stein Mart paper bags used for merchandise purchases. The bags would then be given to the newspaper, where the advertising staff there would convert the drawings into advertising copy. By the early 1980s, these newspaper advertisements shifted first from focusing on the fact that the merchandise came from Saks to promoting specific brand names such as Calvin Klein, Christian Dior, and Pierre Cardin. It then changed further to more polished ads with photos and tasteful drawings that did not mention specific products, but rather attempted to create an image of "high quality merchandise" delivered in "our warm and pleasant atmosphere." Advertisements invited customers to "Discover Stein Mart...a variety of finer things on sale every day."

Allen continued this image-building marketing focus, and tried to align Stein Mart's advertising approach with the company's strategy to target a specific customer segment that normally shopped in department stores. What attracted these shoppers to Stein Mart? Stein Mart's appeal centered on offering name-brand merchandise, with a fashion look, at a great price. So, with the help of an ad agency, the company developed a new slogan — and one that it would use for more than a decade — "The Name, The Look, The Price." As Allen explained the message, "If you're looking for the name, we got the brands. If you're looking for fashion, we got it. But we got it at a price."

One of the obstacles to achieving this upscale image was the company's name. Allen recalls, "I'll never forget when we opened the first Texas store. . . . I went to look at the site. Driving down the road, looking at who was in the area, I never saw so many different outlets with the word "Mart" after it. . . . There was Tire Mart, Laundry Mart, Wal-Mart, and K-Mart. It was like 'Mart City', so when you see Stein Mart, we originally had people thinking that we sold drink containers. Because the other 'Marts' were so specialized. Tire Mart sold tires, and Furniture Mart sold furniture. So Stein Mart..." Allen even suggested that the company change its name, but Jay, while realizing that keeping "Mart" might run counter to the more upscale image he hoped to foster, did not want to do that.

Allen introduced the use of focus groups to help the company develop marketing strategies, and the issue of the Stein Mart name came up in these sessions. What Allen found surprising were the responses to the question, "When you think of Stein Mart, what do you think of?" Very different responses came from "blind" (comprised of people who did not know the store or had never been in one) and "non-blind" (comprised of people who had been in the stores) groups. For the non-customers, since all "Marts" seemed to be associated with a product identity, there was more of a product name focus. But for customers, the Stein Mart name oftentimes meant quality merchandise and outstanding customer service.

It became evident that as the company expanded, it had developed a growing group of loyal customers, and these customers were making Stein Mart successful. Despite all of the sophisticated systems and improved controls implemented during the 1980s, top management of the company realized that it couldn't have happened without dedicated employees, and the enthusiasm and level of customer service that they brought to the stores every day. As Jack Williams observed, "One of my early mentors when I first got into business said, 'Surround yourself with good people and let them do their jobs.' We are very fortunate; we surround ourselves with some very good people." The company tried to foster a family-oriented culture, one that genuinely cared about its employees. And this attitude started with Jay, who explained, "We like people, we appreciate people, and we thank people. I don't have a more important part to my job than thanking the people that contribute to the success of our company. And their contribution is great! The day we lose sight of that or take it for granted, the company is in big trouble."[4]

This emphasis on the important role played by its employees, or associates, was reinforced by a number of programs established to acknowledge individual contributions. Every month, a "mystery shopper" visited each store to rate that store on customer service. The mystery shopper identified associates who gave especially outstanding service and these associates received not only a certificate of recognition, but also a cash award. In addition, each store recognized an associate of the month and an associate of the year, important morale builders and part of a successful effort to reduce employee turnover and make associates feel like part of the Stein Mart family.

Stein Mart not only focused on being a caring employer, but also being a good community citizen. Like his father, Jay had a strong belief in community service, and the need to give something back. After returning home from college, Jay became active in the Greenville Chamber of Commerce, Salvation Army, and other local civic organizations. Once he moved his company and his family to Jacksonville, Jay transferred his energy and commitment to his new community. As Jay often commented, "To whom much is given, much is expected, and that's the creed I live by." He became a major supporter of the arts and served on the board of the Cummer Gallery of Art and the Jacksonville Symphony Orchestra, as well as being active with the Jacksonville Chamber of Commerce and chairing the Sheriff's Advisory Board. He even joined the board of The Bolles School, despite the bad memories of his student days spent there. Jack Williams also took an active role at the Chamber of Commerce and its Committee of 100, an economic development group. Jack chaired the local Dreams Come True, a nonprofit organization that helped to fulfill the dreams of terminally ill children. Both Jay and Jack encouraged other Stein Mart executives and associates to become active in the community, and certainly led by example.

As a company, Stein Mart continued a very successful charitable-giving promotion begun years earlier in Memphis. Each store would select a local charity and on the day after Thanksgiving — the busiest sales day during the entire year for retailers — would donate 10 percent of its sales to that organization. In Jacksonville, which by mid-1990 had three stores, Stein Mart had designated the Jacksonville Symphony, Wolfson Children's Hospital, the Jacksonville Zoo, and others for this annual donation. And Stein Mart stores in other cities selected worthy causes in their communities to receive contributions.

This corporate commitment to community involvement helped Stein Mart be selected as the 1990 First Coast Company of the Year. The award was especially gratifying to Jay because it was based on the assessments of his fellow CEOs from the fifty largest privately-owned companies in Jacksonville and surrounding "First Coast" counties. Taking into consideration company history, company growth, and community involvement, the award recognized that Stein Mart had become, in only a short time, a leader in its new headquarters community.

✳ ✳ ✳ ✳ ✳

By the end of the 1980s, Stein Mart had become a far different company than it had been at the start of the decade. Its stores carried a consistent selection of upscale, brand-name merchandise, offered at prices generally 25 to 60 percent below that charged by traditional department and specialty stores. The company could assure these bargain prices because of its strong vendor relationships, first developed by Jay and then continued by an expanding group of professional buyers, and by the implementation of systems designed to ensure efficient inventory handling. The network of stores had standardized floor plans and a standardized look, which provided a distinctive ambiance designed to appeal to upscale customers. There was only one exception to this new Stein Mart, and that was Store No. 1 in Greenville, Mississippi.

The Greenville store was different, and Jay let his father continue to run it any way he wanted. The corporate staff in Jacksonville knew that Store No. 1 had been placed off-limits. If a company buyer had the opportunity to acquire some end-of-season merchandise as part of a larger purchase, he could ask if the Greenville store had any interest. If unsold, slow-moving merchandise remained in some of the other stores, it could be offered to the Greenville store at a special price. But no one in Jacksonville could dictate what merchandise Greenville carried. Jake continued to

make his own merchandising decisions, and he and Freda continued to take their own buying trips, although Jay often asked Larry Shelton to go along to help his elderly parents. The merchandise selection in the Greenville store continued to be different from that in any other Stein Mart. The layout and arrangement of the store remained unique. It followed a different process for receiving merchandise and declined to install a number of system-wide controls and reporting requirements. The original Greenville Stein Mart remained rooted in its past.

48. Jake Stein with his granddaughter, Jay Meredith.

But the Greenville store continued to make money. Jake Stein knew his customers, and understood what merchandise they could afford. Nevertheless, remaining profitable in downtown Greenville became increasingly difficult. The Greenville Mall opened in the early 1970s, and J. C. Penney and Sears Roebuck quickly relocated to this new mall on Highway 1. Soon afterwards, Wal-Mart and K-Mart opened big stores on the outskirts of town, and the downtown merchants began to struggle. Their difficulties only increased when the city completed an ill-advised downtown renovation project that converted Washington Avenue, the principal downtown shopping location, from a two-way, four-lane road to a one-way, serpentine street that discouraged people from driving downtown to shop.

By the mid-1980s, most of the old-time family-owned stores that had been on Washington Avenue for years had gone out of business. The once vibrant downtown shopping district now had a surplus of vacant and abandoned storefronts. In early November 1987, Bernie Stein announced that the Sam Stein store would close. Bernie told the *Delta Democrat-Times*, "I've been in the business for fifty-five years and I hate to do it, but it's time to call it quits." He said that the store had suffered a significant loss of volume during the past three years and, at that rate, would be bankrupt in another two or three years. Sam Stein's going-out-of-business sale continued until February 1988, when it finally closed its doors.

Sam Stein's closed, but Bernie, at the age of sixty-nine, needed something to do. Several months later, he leased a small store on Highway 1, about a mile from the Greenville Mall, and opened a men's clothing store, Sam Stein's Big & Tall. Bernie admitted that he hadn't opened the store to make a lot of money, only to cover expenses and keep busy. Julius Sherman would come to the store whenever he wanted, just because he too had nothing else to do. Bernie's son, Robert, started working at the store in late 1989 when his father became ill, and Robert continued operating Sam Stein's Big & Tall until October 2002.

With the closing of Sam Stein's, Stein Mart remained one of the few stores still open downtown. By the late 1980s, however, Jake's health had begun to fail. He spent less and less time at the store, leaving the day-to-day supervision to his long-time store manager, Claude Beck. While Jake battled cancer, he received a number of tributes recognizing his business successes and community involvement. In April 1988, Governor Ray Mabus presented Jake with the Governor's Economic Excellence Award. On the local level, Greenville's *Delta Democrat-Times* instituted a new Community Achievement Award, and named Jake as its first recipient in January 1989. Jake was too ill to attend the awards ceremony, but Freda and Jay accepted the plaque that paid him tribute. The plaque read, "For his commitment to brotherhood and dignity of all people, and his years of silent service for the betterment of Greenville." The publisher of the newspaper announced that this annual award in future years would be called the Jake Stein Community Achievement Award.

The following month, Jake Stein died on February 28, 1989. He was buried in Greenville's Jewish cemetery, in a family plot near his sister Sadie. Within a year, Bernie Stein would pass away and be buried next to his brother, the two of them finally at peace with each other.

49. *Jack Williams and Jay Stein. This photograph was taken for Stein Mart's 2002 Annual Report. In his message to shareholders, Jay recognized Jack's retirement and expressed "my appreciation to my friend, my partner, and my co-worker, Jack Williams. Jack began with us almost at the beginning, when we had just three stores. I want to thank him for his sincere love, wise counsel, and tireless devotion to this company and me. We are, in great part, the Company we are today because Jack Williams answered my call 23 years ago."*

CHAPTER 5

The National Retailer

"What is Stein Mart?... The best description of Stein Mart was coined by a reporter in South Florida who had just seen our Boca Raton store for the first time. She labeled Stein Mart a 'hybrid' — a cross between a department store or a specialty shop, and an off-price retailer. When you walk in, it feels like a department store — merchandise is displayed and accessorized in lifestyle groupings, the labels are familiar to discerning shoppers, and sales associates are knowledgeable and professional. But when you examine the price tag, you find prices on par with an off-price retailer. Our customers tell us it's the best of both worlds, and we like to think so, too.

"Stein Mart has it roots in my hometown, Greenville, Mississippi. My grandfather, and later my father, grew a small store in downtown Greenville into the largest department store in the Delta. While Stein Mart has moved away from its original roots as a department store over the years, it has never wavered from our family retailing philosophy: give our customers something special. At Stein Mart, something special is in-season, top-quality fashion at discounted prices."

– Jay Stein, from a Presentation to J.C. Bradford's Institutional Equity Conference, February 15, 1994

*A*s Stein Mart expanded and prospered in the late 1980s, Jay Stein began pondering how to best finance the company's future growth. He and Jack Williams held numerous discussions about the available alternatives — to interest private individuals in making equity investments in the company; to become an "operating partner" with a retailing chain, retaining the company's name and some operating autonomy within a larger corporate entity; or to take the company public by selling stock through an IPO (initial public offering).

While Stein Mart's executives evaluated these various options, the retail merchandising industry faced some difficult times. In January 1986, in its "Annual Report on American Industry," *Forbes* observed that "for most retailers, their traditionally competitive business has never been rougher." According to the *Forbes* analysis: "What seems to be happening goes beyond the periodic discounting wave retailers have always been afflicted with and suggests a sea change in American shopping habits. Many Americans are happy to shop in huge concrete-floored warehouses to get a better price, but they also want to be pampered with lots of attention in specialty shops."[1] For many retailers — and especially the large department store chains — this retail merchandising environment only got tougher during the next several years. The 1970s and 1980s had witnessed excessive construction of new shopping centers and enclosed malls, and now overcapacity in the number of retail outlets confronted a slowdown in consumer spending and a softening economy. By the end of the decade, there existed an estimated eighteen square feet of retail space for every man, woman, and child in the country, more than double the amount of 1972. Meanwhile, sales per square feet (adjusted for inflation) had begun to decline. A *Newsweek* article in the summer of 1988 entitled "Retailing's Hard Times" focused on large-scale layoffs as business slowed. "Store sales have been soft for months," *Newsweek* reported. "Some trace the slowdown to last year's miniskirt. It never really caught on, and that kept a lot of women (and their pocketbooks) out of stores. That may be too facile an answer, but fashion drives department-store sales, and women simply aren't buying much these days, be it mini, maxi, or something in between."[2]

Department stores throughout the country faced intense competition from aggressive new rivals: discounters like Wal-Mart; specialty stores like Nordstrom's and Victoria's Secret; so-called "category killers" like Toys "R" Us and Circuit City; and catalogue merchants like Land's End and L. L. Bean. And many of the large department store chains seemed unable to adapt to the new realities of the 1980s because of the internal management focus caused by a spate of mergers and acquisitions and divestitures. Many lost touch with their customers as their emphasis shifted from marketing and merchandising to debt service coverage and maintenance of the financial ratios required by the banks that financed the acquisitions. These corporate takeovers included London-based British American Tobacco's purchase of Marshall Fields and the Australian Hooker Corporation's acquisition of the B. Altman & Company chain. But the wheeling-and-dealing reached its height (or, perhaps more accurately, its nadir) with Canadian real estate developer Robert Campeau acquiring first Allied Stores in 1986, and then two years later Federated Department Stores. Both transactions were so-called LBOs, or leveraged buyouts, which had become quite popular among Wall Street investment bankers. Campeau bought both chains — which included such well-known stores as Bloomingdale's, Abraham & Straus, Rich's, Burdines, and Jordan Marsh — with minimal cash and huge amounts of debt. Theoretically, this indebtedness could be repaid by profitably divesting selected businesses and by bringing in new management to improve productivity and store performance. It did not work, in part because of Campeau's inept managerial abilities and in part because of the weak economy and the increasingly competitive retail environment. By early 1990, Campeau's disastrously overpriced acquisitions had spiraled downward into bankruptcy court.[3]

Stein Mart benefited from the operating woes of the department store chains, at least in those Southeastern markets where they had stores. It was during this period that Jay, Jack, and Mason Allen had specifically identified department store shoppers as its target customers, and had begun directing its image-building marketing efforts toward this customer segment. In many ways, Stein Mart's operating strategies fit well with the changing nature of consumer shopping habits. Shoppers wanted quality merchandise at affordable prices, delivered with excellent customer service — all part of the Stein Mart shopping experience. Fewer women — many of whom now worked — had the time for leisurely browsing through shopping malls. Instead, they wanted convenience and a quicker shopping experience, which they could find at Stein Mart stores located in community shopping centers (as opposed to shopping malls) with ample nearby parking.

Stein Mart managed to gain new customers from the struggling department stores. Nevertheless, the weak retailing environment, the slowing economy, and the publicity surrounding so many prominent retailers heading for bankruptcy threatened to complicate Stein Mart's search for an equity infusion as Jay held informal discussions with a number of companies and individuals. Jay realized the need for additional outside equity, but these preliminary inquiries left him uneasy about surrendering control of the company. According to Jay, "We frankly never felt that we wanted a single individual partner at the time, and we certainly did not want to lose control of the business. So after exploring a number of private ventures, we decided that the public route was better." Once the decision had been made to pursue an IPO, Mason Allen recalls that management "had a two- or three-year period where we said we have to look at it as the public would look at the company, and what do we need to do in that period of time to package it."

Stein Mart's management team began making some organizational changes to better position itself to meet the expectations of Wall Street investors. In December 1989, Jay replaced his late father as chairman of Stein Mart, Inc., with Jack becoming president and chief operating officer. For years, Stein Mart's board of directors had been largely a family board, consisting of Jay, his wife, his parents, Jack Williams, and family attorney Frank Hunger. As the company prepared for its IPO, Jay named Mason Allen to the board and added several prominent Jacksonville business executives — Albert D. Ernest, president of Barnett Banks, Inc; James H. Winston, an insurance and real estate executive; and Robert Davis, former chairman of Winn-Dixie, Inc. The company also tried to strengthen management — especially in the finance area, which would be critical during an IPO — hiring Donald B. Williams as senior vice president/ finance and administration.

The company selected First Boston Corp. as the lead underwriter and in early 1992 filed the required registration statement with the Securities and Exchange Commission. According to its filing, Stein Mart planned to sell 4.6 million shares of stock at $14 to $16 per share. It hoped to raise $64.4 million to $73.6 million. These funds would pay Jay and his wife Cindy, who owned all of the privately-held company stock, a dividend equivalent to their equity in the company. It also would repay the company's bank debt and provide funds for financing its expansion program. When Stein Mart announced its IPO in mid-March, the stock market was bullish and a number of companies had recently completed successful equity offerings. Unfortunately, five weeks later the market had weakened, and First Boston scaled back the offering. On April 22, 1992, Stein Mart went public with the sale of

50. The first Board of Directors for Stein Mart as a public company, as pictured in the 1992 Annual Report. In the back row, from the left, Mitchell W. Legler, James H. Winston, Robert D. Davis and Albert Ernest, Jr.; in the front, from the left, John H. Williams, Jr., Jay Stein, and Mason Allen.

3.25 million shares at $13 each. After paying the underwriters, $30.5 million of the proceeds from the IPO went to Jay and his wife, who still retained a 75 percent ownership of the company, with the remainder used to repay $9.9 million of the company's approximate $12 million debt. Nevertheless, by year-end, internally generated funds had resulted in no term debt and a revolving credit facility with a zero balance.

Even though the IPO had not generated as much equity as originally planned — and no additional moneys to finance expansion of its store network — interest in the company among investors increased during the next year, with Stein Mart's stock price rising from its initial $13 per share to $32 by mid-1993. Investor enthusiasm for Stein Mart reflected not only its solid financial performance — with a reported 23.5 percent sales increase for 1992 and a $13.9 million, or 92 cents per share, profit for its first year as a public company — but also an aggressive effort by Jay and Jack to tell the Stein Mart story to Wall Street analysts and potential investors.

Throughout the remainder of 1992 and during the next several years, Jay and Jack attended countless investor conferences to introduce Stein Mart and to explain what made the company unique. At a typical investor presentation, Jay would begin by talking about the "four critical elements" in a Stein Mart store — the discounted prices, the premium service, the merchandise presentation, and the high quality of not only the merchandise, but also store personnel and the shopping environment. Expressing a "frustration…at trying to communicate the essence of Stein Mart" to audiences where few had ever been inside one of the stores, Jay would give a "tour" of a typical store, using a slide show or a company-prepared video. Then Jack would present a recap of Stein Mart's financial performance and expansion plans, together with outlining how the company kept a tight control on expenses.

These presentations obviously worked, as a number of investment firms began to follow Stein Mart with "buy" ratings. Typical was the initial investment analyst report from Alex. Brown & Sons that described Stein Mart stores as "a visual delight, distinguished by smooth department-to-department adjacencies, clean sight lines, and confident selections of merchandise arranged by lifestyle. The Company is further differentiated by its intensive focus on customer service, something particularly evident in Stein Mart's upscale designer 'Boutiques.'" With Stein Mart's stock price soaring, Jay used the opportunity to diversify his own financial position by selling 2.5 million shares of his own stock in a subsequent offering the year after the IPO.

As a public company, Stein Mart executives had to spend time courting the investment community and crafting careful responses to inquiries from Wall Street analysts. But the company's main focus remained on the customer, and the merchandise, and managing the expanding network of stores. In 1992, Stein Mart opened seven new stores, and closed its first under-performing one. In 1993, it opened fifteen, including its first stores in the major metropolitan areas of Houston and Atlanta, as well as expanding into the North with store openings in Cincinnati and Dayton, Ohio. Fourteen more stores opened in 1994, and twenty in 1995, when the company achieved the milestone of opening its one hundredth store. Thereafter, Stein Mart's expansion program involved more than twenty openings every year, with a high of thirty-two new stores in 1998.

Stein Mart's growth placed a strain on the company's infrastructure. On the merchandising side, Mason Allen already had been building a deep, experienced staff of buyers. He continued to expand his staff to match the increasing number of stores and to develop better tools for monitoring inventory levels and merchandising needs. On the operational side, Jack Williams had been more reluctant to add staff. Jack describes the organizational structure of the early 1990s as follows: "In those days, Jay had Mason reporting to him, and everybody else reported to me." The expanded responsibilities caused by becoming a public company necessitated a revaluation. Shortly after the IPO, Jay asked one of the new directors, Bob Davis (of the Davis family that founded Winn-Dixie, which for years had been a publicly-traded company) to visit Jack and to talk with him about the need "to turn loose" some of his responsibilities.

Jack agreed that he needed to delegate more. First, he sought to relieve himself of some of his real estate responsibilities, hiring two experienced commercial real estate professionals, Andy Hoffheimer and David Darr, to be tenant reps for the eastern and western sections of the country. Their jobs involved studying the demographics of potential expansion target cities and doing all of the legwork to identify and prescreen potential store sites. To oversee the real estate area, in early 1993, Jack hired W. Michael Allen, an attorney who had worked for a shopping center developer in Jacksonville. Allen assumed responsibility for all property management and for coordinating with landlords. Initially, Jack continued his involvement with negotiating store leases. He had developed a reputation as a tough, effective negotiator, committed to keeping the company's real estate costs relatively low when compared to other upscale retailers. Mike Allen provided the legal expertise needed to close these transactions, but gradually the lease negotiation responsibilities shifted to Allen, who in 1995 was promoted to vice president/real estate.

Jack soon began recruiting experienced executives to upgrade other key positions on the operations and corporate staff. Having Stein Mart now a publicly-traded company made management recruiting easier, in part because of the ability to offer stock option incentives. In February 1992, just months before the IPO, the company had set up a stock option plan, and Jay awarded options to more than one hundred key employees. Participation in the stock option plan included store managers and merchandise buyers, and became an important factor in the company's low turnover rate at the management level. From its inception, this stock option plan was recognized as an attractive incentive to recruit additional talent to the company.

In the summer of 1993, Jack hired Michael D. Fisher to be the company's first director of stores, thus relieving himself of direct responsibility for supervising the company's regional directors. Shortly afterwards, D. Hunt Hawkins, who had previously worked for Genesco, joined the company as senior vice president/human resources. Hawkins focused his efforts on improving training and management development programs, instituting new compensation and employee benefit plans, and developing the internal infrastructure necessary to oversee a system-wide employee base that would soon number 10,000 associates. Several years later, Jack upgraded the finance area by hiring James G. Delfs, an experienced executive from The Limited, Inc., and Helzberg Diamonds, to be senior vice president and chief financial officer. Delfs worked to implement more sophisticated financial and audit controls and to improve financial reporting communications with the investment community.

Of these new members of Stein Mart's management team, none faced greater challenges than the new director of stores, Michael Dean Fisher. He had been raised in Tampa and then attended the University of Florida, where he majored in advertising. After a tour of duty as a Navy pilot, Fisher returned home to Tampa in 1974 and joined Maas Brothers' executive training program. After several years with Maas Brothers, Fisher had the opportunity to become an assistant manager at a new Tampa store being opened by Robinson's, the Florida division of Associated Dry Goods Corporation. At Robinson's, he progressed to assistant controller, senior vice president for management information systems (MIS), and eventually director of stores for its seven Florida outlets. He stayed with Robinson's through Associated Dry Goods' acquisition by the May Company. When the May Company subsequently made the corporate decision to exit Florida, it sold its Florida-based stores to Maison Blanche and transferred Fisher to its Cleveland division. In 1988, Fisher joined California-based Miller's Outpost, a retail chain that sold young men's and young women's active sportswear at stores located throughout the West.

Fisher describes retailing as "a network business," and he learned about the new position at Stein Mart from Michael Remsen, an old friend from college and Maas Brothers who now happened to be a divisional merchandising manager at Stein Mart. No Stein Marts had been opened on the West Coast, and Fisher knew very little about the company. But he did want to move his family back to Florida, and it sounded like an intriguing opportunity. Fisher had several interviews with Jack Williams, and it became clear to him that the principal issue confronting the company involved building the infrastructure necessary to support growing by twenty to thirty new stores per year. Having been the director of stores for Miller's Outpost, which had multiple divisions and more than 400 mall and non-mall stores, Fisher felt confident that he "had a perspective on how to manage a large network of stores." He evidently convinced Jack Williams, because Jack hired him as executive vice president with responsibility for overall direction of the growing store network.

Fisher began his new position in August 1993 and spent his first three months "in the field," asking a lot of questions and assessing the talent level. He concluded that an additional level of management would be needed to supervise the stores, and he set out to meet that need by appointing a number of district directors with responsibility for ten to thirteen stores. They would be expected to spend four days a week, every week, out in the field, visiting each store at least once every three weeks. These district directors would report to the regional directors, who now received larger geographic areas to supervise.

Most of the district directors came from internal promotions, selected from the pool of successful store managers. But Fisher wanted to ensure that the company did not become too incestuous, and he insisted that some new district director openings be filled by outsiders who had different perspectives from their experiences at other retail chains so as "to infuse some new processes, new ideas." Fisher did maintain, however, the company policy begun by Jay and Jack with the 1981 opening of Store No. 5 that all new store managers be internal hires from the ranks of assistant store managers who had been trained in the Stein Mart way of doing business. Fisher sought to improve this process, working with the new HR director Hunt Hawkins to develop better training programs and to implement more formal

performance evaluations that not only tied incentive plans to quanti-
tative sales performance and store shrinkage goals, but also included
less measurable qualitative leadership and management development
components.

Fisher also worked with Mason Allen to establish formal protocols
to improve the process for communicating needs from the stores to the
merchandising organization, and for communicating the merchandising vision from the buyers to the stores. To Fisher, a two-way "communications conduit that allows the messages to go in both directions, and
some processes in place and some discipline in place to be sure that both
sides are listening" represented a critical component to ensuring success.
He found that Allen agreed with that approach, and consequently not
a lot of "operational versus merchandising problems" developed. Fisher
gives much of the credit for that to Jay and Jack, who simply would not
allow for such friction. Instead, he observed "a propensity for teamwork"
in the company's culture. "One of Stein Mart's great strengths," Fisher
observes, "is that there is a cultural dynamic which not only encourages
teamwork, but won't tolerate the dissent that may normally occur in a
merchandising organization."

While Mike Fisher worked to refine the management approaches
necessary to oversee a network of stores that grew to 100 by 1995 and
205 by 1999 — stretching from New York to California — countless
other initiatives were underway throughout the company. New technology allowed the company to automate its merchandise planning and
budgeting systems. Price scanning "wands" installed in every store not
only expedited customer checkout procedures, but also communicated
with the company's computerized inventory-tracking system to initiate
automatic reorders of regularly stocked items. The company revamped
its merchandising receiving systems. With approximately 90 percent
of its merchandise being shipped from manufacturers directly to each
store, without passing through a central distribution center, these new
processes allowed merchandise to be more quickly checked-in, ticketed,
and moved to the sales floor.

In addition to these numerous operating and merchandising
initiatives, the company continued its aggressive store expansion program. The estimated cost of opening a prototype new store — fixtures,
equipment, leasehold improvements, and pre-opening advertising and

51. *Advertisement for the opening of Stein Mart's 100th store in Savannah, Georgia, November 17, 1995.*

training — ranged from $450,000 to $650,000 per store, plus an initial inventory investment of approximately $1 million. Stein Mart financed all of these openings, plus improvements to existing stores and information systems enhancements, from internally generated funds, choosing to reinvest its profits to fund these initiatives rather than paying dividends or incurring debt. The company reported annual capital expenditures from current cash flow of between $11.5 million and $19.7 million during the years 1993 though 1997.

Despite these heavy infrastructure expenditures, Stein Mart remained highly profitable during these years. Net sales grew from $342.7 million in 1993 to $792.7 million in 1997, with profits increasing from $16.7 million (or 70 cents per share, restated to reflect the three-for-two stock split in September 1993) to $34.8 million ($1.47 per share) in 1997. Only in 1995 did the company show a negative trend, when profits declined slightly by two cents per share during a sluggish year for all retailers, or as the company's Annual Report wryly observed, "our earnings progress was impeded by a prevailing atmosphere of indifference on the part of the consumer."

Even though Stein Mart delivered solid operating earnings and maintained a strong, debt-free balance sheet, some Wall Street analysts, after initially promoting its stock, soured on the company. Part of this negativism reflected Wall Street's general lack of enthusiasm for the retailing industry, which from 1993 through 1995 seemed to be suffering from too many stores, too little consumer spending, and what one analyst called "an extended period of fashion drought." Jay and Jack both grew frustrated in their dealings with the analysts. While they had always viewed department stores and specialty shops as the company's principal competitors, many analysts could never accept that Stein Mart did not fit the profile of the typical off-price discounter and instead chose to compare Stein Mart with Ross, T.J. Maxx, and Marshall's. Stein Mart also experienced difficulty meeting the demands of investment analysts for in-depth disclosures of sales trends and other business performance measurements. Many analysts wanted monthly sales results, but Jack never thought that to be a good indicator of performance, since monthly sales figures didn't take into account advertising campaigns, special sales, and other factors that impacted profitability. Instead, he only provided quarterly sales figures, later admitting that "we got a lot of flak from analysts that you're not giving us anything to work with." Also, Stein Mart in the mid-1980s had switched its fiscal year-end (FYE) to December 31 when it changed its corporate structure to a Subchapter-S Corporation. Thus, its quarterly and year-end financial results did not compare easily to other retailers who had a more typical January 31 FYE.

Relations with several investment analysts became strained in 1995. Early that year, the analyst for Smith Barney lowered her rating of the

When is a Mart not a mart?
When it's a Stein Mart.

A store that doesn't just unseat perceptions,
it pulls the chair right out.

Today's current fashion from the famous names you know, for women, men and children. Shoes and accessories, unique and special gifts, linens and things for the home...all with a price tag of 25% to 60% less than other stores' every day. And although we keep our prices nice and low, you'll find our standards very high. Our elegant stores are easy to shop, our merchandise beautifully displayed, and our associates are there just to make you happy. We like to think that knowing about Stein Mart is a bit like knowing a special little secret.

You could pay more. But you'll have to go somewhere else.®

52. *Promotional brochure that asks, "When is a Mart not a mart?"*

company from "buy" to "neutral" as sales in comparable stores failed to meet expectations. She complained that Stein Mart's management had developed plans that were "not clearly indicated to the Street.... We believe that the company will lose investors' confidence in the go-forward earnings projections and that the stock will become a show-me story." Several months later, an analyst for Raymond James took an even more strident tone as he commented on quarterly earnings "below our expectations." The explanation pointedly criticized the company's sharing of financial data: "Our opinions are based on bits and scraps of information . . . In other words, the information flow from this company is not what we might hope for. The company is in large measure still run as a private company, with very little material provided for what we would consider in-depth analysis. We believe that most of it is intentionally withheld."

While Stein Mart's stock price fell as analysts voiced criticism of the company's financial reporting, company executives became annoyed by Wall Street's short-term focus and by the tendency of investment bankers to lump all retailers together when economic times got tough. Jack explains, "The retail business is cyclical. When you have a down cycle and you are a privately-held company and you are still profitable, you don't have to talk about it. It's nobody's business. You certainly would talk with the bankers that you had credit lines with, but they understood. . . . That was one of the hardest things for me to understand and accept back in 1993, 1994, 1995 when we went through that retail down cycle. I can remember being at some analyst conference and at the Q & A getting questions with the implications that 'you're all a bunch of dirty dogs' because the profitability rate has dropped. I remember being a little bit incensed, but at the same time astute enough to turn it back on them. 'If I were an investor right now, I would take comfort in this. We have been through a down retail cycle and you've learned what the downside is, and the downside isn't so bad because we're still profitable.'"

After a slight drop in 1995 earnings that disappointed both management and Wall Street, Stein Mart bounced back in 1996 and 1997. It reported robust growth and strong earnings, and company executives made extra efforts to tell Wall Street of these successes. Stein Mart's record 1997 earnings of $1.47 per share helped to raise the company's stock price from a $9.63 low during the first quarter of 1995 to a high of $33.75 in mid-1997. When adjusted for the stock split several years earlier, this stock price represented a nearly 40 percent increase over its post-IPO high in late 1993. Not coincidently, mid-1997 saw Mason Allen decide to take early retirement at the age of fifty-four. Jay had been generous in granting stock options to Allen, and this proved to be a propitious time for him to try some consulting and to pursue some personal interests.

To replace Allen, Jay named Michael Remsen as the new executive vice president/merchandising. Remsen had been with Stein Mart for five years and had done an exceptional job as the general merchandise manager in charge of buying ladies' sportswear and children's clothing. Unfortunately, like the case of Allen's two predecessors, Remsen never before had been a chief merchandising officer, which can be a high-risk position when fashion trends shift and merchandising buys miss the mark. Problems developed during the first half of 1998 in two key areas, the men's division and the Boutique, where Jack Williams noted "badly received fashion merchandise... had to be heavily promoted and deeply discounted." As the company tried to recover its "loss of momentum in the shopping habits of our core customers," many areas of the country where Stein Mart had stores experienced unusual weather patterns, first an unseasonably warm fall and then paralyzing ice and snow storms during those critical shopping days before and after Christmas. As a result, Stein Mart reported a sharp drop in profits from $34.8 million (or 73 cents per share, restated to reflect a two-for-one stock split in April of 1998) the preceding year to $20.5 million (44 cents per share) for 1998. In their letter to shareholders in the Annual Report, Jay and Jack commented, "Merchandising errors, coupled with unusual weather patterns in the last half of the year, forced increased markdowns in 1998, thereby eroding gross margins." They promised that after a review of "every aspect of our business," changes had been made "to re-capture our customer by emphasizing the foundations of our Company's concept: namely, an upscale product at a price that represents true value."

But it did not happen in 1999. Gross sales margin declined, inventory turnover slowed, large markdowns continued, and operating expenses increased. During the fourth quarter of the year, the company announced a pre-tax $20.5 million charge to earnings related to closing ten under-performing stores, covering the costs of lease terminations and losses from liquidation sales of merchandise. Stein Mart's earnings for the year fell to $11.8 million (26 cents per share), and the company's stock reached a low of $4.88. Although a number of external factors can be cited as contributing to the 1998-99 downturn, Jay and Jack chose to use these difficult times as an opportunity to reevaluate the company's management and organizational structure, and to initiate those strategies necessary to get Stein Mart ready for the challenges of the new twenty-first century.

* * * * *

As the 1990s drew to a close, Stein Mart had more than 200 stores in twenty-eight states and more than 12,000 associates. The company had positioned itself as a distinctive off-price retailer, with a unique strategy for attracting middle- and upper-class customers. It sold quality brand-name and fashion clothing for men, women, and children, together with accessories, gifts, linens, and shoes, in an upscale ambiance similar to that found in better department stores, with wide aisles, attractive merchandise displays, and attentive customer service. But, when compared to department stores, it sold this merchandise at prices 20 to 60 percent lower. As one of its advertising slogans in the mid-1990s proclaimed, "You could pay more. But you'll have to go somewhere else." And in 1999, net sales topped $1 billion for the first time in company history.

Stein Mart had come a long way in the thirty-five years that had passed since Jake Stein opened the expanded, and newly renamed, Stein Mart in November 1964. But the company's roots remained in Greenville, Mississippi. Jay Stein might travel in different circles — addressing Wall Street analysts in New York City; accompanying Vice President Al Gore to Poland to commemorate the fiftieth anniversary of the Warsaw ghetto uprising; traveling to Washington, D.C., for meetings of the board of trustees for the John F. Kennedy Center for the Performing Arts — but he still had a soft spot for Greenville. He would travel to Greenville frequently to visit his mother, who insisted on continuing to work at the original store. Jay enjoyed visiting the store, where he knew the employees by name and had worked side-by-side with many of them years earlier. One of them, Rose Whittington, had started working at Sam Stein's in 1943, before Jay had been born, and "Miss Rose" remained at the store on the 200 block of Washington Avenue for fifty-three years. She remembers when Jay was too young to work, but would come to the store to play — and she would bring her dog from home and help young Jay rearrange the chairs in the shoe department so that he and "Spotty" had a play area. Now in the 1990s, Miss Rose and the other associates at Store No. 1 still looked forward to Jay's visits.

The Greenville store had a special status in the company, but as the Stein Mart organization changed, Greenville lagged behind. While Jake Stein lived, the corporate staff in Jacksonville left him alone. He had full control over the merchandise carried in the store, including how to price it and promote it. Jake was not upscale, but neither were his long-time customers, so the Greenville store continued to cater to the less affluent. After Jake died, the company slowly began to bring the original Stein Mart into closer conformity with other Stein Mart stores. It needed repainting, and new carpeting and fixtures. The corporate buyers from Jacksonville began to purchase more merchandise for the store, although it continued to have a less upscale emphasis. Larry Shelton, in addition to his other corporate responsibilities, had been given the assignment of helping with the merchandising of Store No. 1. He accompanied Jake and Freda on buying trips in the late 1980s, and after Jake's death continued to go on buying trips specifically for the Greenville store and continued to maintain relationships with Jake's long-time vendors. He and Bob Brooks, the regional director responsible for the store, worked through "the process of marrying the two merchandise mixes together."

53. *Carl Davis, Bob Brooks, and Larry Shelton at the 25th anniversary of the opening of the Memphis store, September 2002. Brooks, like Davis and Shelton, had worked at Shainberg's before joining Stein Mart in 1983 as assistant manager of Store No. 9 in New Orleans. In 1987, Brooks became one of the first regional directors of stores and has continued as a regional director for the past sixteen years.*

Jake Stein always said that he would never move his store out of the downtown area, but by the mid-1990s downtown Greenville had become a depressed area. Hopes for a downtown economic revival focused not on rebuilding a strong retailing presence, but rather on promoting tourism as several casino gambling boats opened on Lake Ferguson, on the other side of the levee across from Stein Mart. Finally, in 1996, Stein Mart closed its downtown store, and relocated Store No. 1 to a new location on Highway 1, across from the Greenville Mall.

As a business decision, relocating Greenville's Stein Mart to the outskirts of town was the right thing to do. But for customers and employees, it proved to be difficult. Many of the store's long-time customers lived downtown and walked to the store. Now they had difficulty getting to the store and, even if they did, the new merchandise selections were not what they wanted. Consequently, after the Greenville store relocated, it began to attract a new set of customers, and the store began to resemble more closely — in terms of merchandise quality and mix, departmental floor plan layout, and general shopping ambiance — the other stores in the Stein Mart network.

Nevertheless, the Greenville store retained a unique "personality." When this author first visited Store No.1 in the spring of 2002, he could sense that there was something different. Walking in the store, one saw the horse and speedboat children's rides in the front, near the cash register stations. People brought their children to the store to have their pictures taken on these rides, the same ones that many remembered riding when they had been children and the Stein store had been located on Washington Avenue. And the rides still worked — although it had become more difficult to find someone to repair them — and still cost only a dime. The store had a gift department filled with merchandise unique among all Stein Mart stores. The gift department remained the domain of Freda Stein. She did all of the gift buying for the Greenville store and, accompanied by Larry Shelton, still went to Atlanta and New York City several times a year to look for those novel items that made her gift department so special. Every day, even though she was then in her late eighties, "Miss Freda" came to the store, charming both customers and employees and making certain that everyone received attentive service.

Despite all of the changes that have transformed Stein Mart, two key concepts can be traced back to Greenville and Store No. 1. First, even though the Stein Mart of today sells a merchandise that is very different from the common, everyday work clothes that Sam and Jake Stein emphasized, the basic business philosophy has not changed. Like his grandfather and father, Jay realizes that to be successful, a retail merchant must offer the customer something different, something of value — and like them, Jay emphasizes that Stein Mart sells quality merchandise at discount prices. The only difference is now that quality merchandise is more upscale, more fashion-oriented, and more directed toward a different group of customers.

Second, the Greenville store was (and still is) a close-knit group of employees, who care about their customers and each other. When you talk with employees from Store No. 1 — and some of them have been there for twenty or thirty years — their personal stories tell how much they care about the company. Their eyes sometimes fill with tears when they talk about Jake Stein and what he meant to them. There is an intense loyalty that many feel toward the Stein family. All of them speak about Stein Mart being a family or "a neighborhood where friends come together." As one of them succinctly described his experience, "Once you got in [hired], you became part of the family. If you're treated good, you have loyalty."

This sense of family, so evident in Store No. 1, has become an essential part of the Stein Mart corporate culture. Defining a corporate culture can be a difficult process, and one often gets very different perspectives depending upon an individual's experiences within the organization. Nevertheless, there is a common thread that seems to emerge, whether talking with sales clerks in Greenville or corporate executives in Jacksonville. As Larry Shelton explains, the company's culture "has evolved over the years, and yet is still the same." He describes the company as "very much like a family." Starting at Stein Mart when he was only twenty-three, he has spent more than half of his lifetime working for the company, and during that time he has developed "a tremendous amount of respect for Jake Stein, Freda Stein, and for Jay Stein. They are very, very fine people. Honest and very dedicated. They're as much family as my own."

Even for those who never knew Jake Stein and joined the company long after it had moved to Jacksonville, there is not only this strong sense of the company as family, but also a realization that the company is committed to providing a family-friendly work environment. Retailing has, in the words of Mike Fisher, "a deservedly bad reputation about being abusive to people. . . . Sixty- or seventy-hour weeks — and eighty-hour weeks during holidays — were not atypical." Stein Mart has made the corporate decision to avoid this approach and to ensure that all associates "be treated with respect." As Hunt Hawkins explains the company's employee relations philosophy, "Our environment is one where we are driven to achieve and we are all goal-oriented, but we feel it can be done without an eighty-hour, high-pressure work week." When asked how that can be accomplished, Hunt responds, "You work smarter. . . . What you find is that you don't necessarily have to be the highest paying to get the loyalty and energy out of the associates to be effective for you. They know that they can still have a family and have a personal life. When they know that, they'll work harder for you for the hours that they are there." Gwen Manto, who joined the company as chief merchandising officer in 2000, describes the Stein Mart culture as one "that combines integrity, entrepreneurism, and respect for people. It includes the ability to support your family in addition to supporting the company." And this family orientation proved to be one of the deciding factors that attracted Manto, a mother of three, to join Stein Mart.

Jay Stein has worked hard to keep this company commitment to caring and family values. Since Stein Mart began expanding by one or two stores per year in the early 1980s, Jay has devoted considerable effort to visiting the stores, spending time with the managers and getting to know the employees. Those closest to him point out that Jay has a genuine concern for associates. During store visits, Jay always makes an effort to reach out to everyone, making sure to visit not only the sales floor but also the backroom areas where the merchandise is received and priced. He brings a message that applies to all associates: "I recognize your importance to the company." And he tries to foster an important corporate theme, that all associates — whether full-time or part-time — have access to him and have access to other senior executives. If someone notices a problem or has a suggestion about how to do something better, Jay and his management team want to know. Jay understands that what makes Stein Mart unique — and what motivates customers to come back again and again — is not just the quality merchandise or low pricing, but exceptional customer service. And this level of service will only be provided by associates who truly care about the customer and who take pride in working at Stein Mart. Dedicated, enthusiastic employees who like their jobs make for satisfied customers.

Jay is what's known as a "people person." He has an outgoing personality far different from his father, one that exudes a warmth and an empathy toward others. He is energized by people, and especially when he is around Stein Mart associates. And when he talks one-on-one with associates, he inspires their confidence and builds loyalty and commitment to the company. During the 1980s and early 1990s, Jay communicated his vision of what Stein Mart should be through frequent personal visits to stores. Michael Ray, who joined Stein Mart as an assistant manager in Little Rock in 1990, remembers Jay coming to that store three or four times during his first year with the company. As the company grew from forty stores in 1990 to several hundred a decade later, visiting every store even once a year became impossible. While Jay still tries to visit several dozen stores each year, today his principal interactions with store managers comes at the annual managers' meeting. Held each March in Orlando, the meeting brings together all store managers and most of the buyers and corporate staff from Jacksonville for a long weekend of business presentations, social activities, and, most importantly, relationship building. It is an opportunity for Jay and other company executives to talk with the managers, hug them for a job well done, and encourage them to face the challenges that lie ahead. According to Hunt Hawkins, who has responsibility for planning and organizing this annual meeting, one of the "key elements" of these meetings "is to reinforce our culture."

Like all organizations that transition from small, locally based, privately held companies to larger, more geographically dispersed, publically traded corporations, Stein Mart has faced the difficult challenges of balancing expansion with trying to maintain its company roots. No longer can that all-important personal touch be delivered exclusively by Jay, or by Jack Williams. Instead, the critical mission of spreading the corporate message of what it means to be part of the Stein Mart organization has passed to the next generation of company executives, one that had been selected and mentored by Jay, Jack, and in later years Mike Fisher. The first level of responsibility for disseminating the corporate culture now rests with the 260 plus store managers, all of whom have come up through the ranks. They are expected to know each of the approximately sixty associates who work in their stores. And the district directors, who should be in each store in their district at least once every three weeks, need to be equally attuned to the needs and problems of associates. According to Mike Ray, who progressed from assistant store manager in 1990 to senior vice president and director of stores in 2001, these district directors and, in turn, the regional directors are "in those stores on a regular basis to feel and sense and see what's going on." They are the direct links between the corporate headquarters in Jacksonville and the stores throughout the country, and they work hard to ensure that Stein Mart remains Stein Mart.

Mike Ray sees yet another unique characteristic that is important to understanding what Stein Mart is. Ray believes that everybody cares about others in the organization, and that "there is a true compassion in the company." He summarizes the company's culture as follows: "You treat people the way you want to be treated.... Part of the culture is that everybody is recognized for being an individual, and everybody is treated individually and fairly and humanely. I think people are empowered. You are responsible for your job in the organization and you are empowered to make the decisions and supported when you need that support.... I've always described part of the culture of the organization as that when somebody comes through the ranks, their hand is down to help the next person to get to that next level. The company has a tremendous history of growing people within the organization."

Teamwork, caring for others, being part of a family — that's what the Stein Mart organization is today. These attitudes are important components of a corporate culture that can be traced back to Greenville, and subsequently nurtured — and in some respects reinvented — by Jay Stein and the management staff that he developed.

* * * * *

As 2000 began, Stein Mart executives felt confident that they had put their operating problems behind them. Under-performing stores had been identified, and Mike Fisher and his regional directors focused on how best to increase productivity and sales at these stores through some combination of adjusting merchandise assortments, improving local visibility through community involvement, and by spending more

54. Stein Mart's senior management team, as pictured in the 2000 Annual Report, with a restored cash register from Greenville Store No. 1 (now on display on the executive floor of the Stein Mart headquarters in Jacksonville). From the left, Jay Stein, Michael D. Fisher, James G. Delfs, Gwen K. Manto, D. Hunt Hawkins, and John H. Williams Jr.

local dollars for advertising and market promotions. Meanwhile, Gwen K. Manto joined the company in February as executive vice president and chief merchandising officer. She had twenty years of experience as a buyer in Atlanta for Macy's and Rich's and then had spent several years in New York as president of Foot Locker Kids. Manto viewed her challenge at Stein Mart as a "turnaround situation" after two disappointing years, and she began to reorganize her merchandising organization. Manto emphasized the importance of keeping "the sizzle" in the merchandise, and she worked closely with the buying staff on color, silhouette, fashion, and those other key factors needed "to make sure we always have great stuff." She focused on improving the planning function responsible for distributing merchandise to each location and began to develop new tools to sort inventory shipments based upon volume, climate, and the psychographic profile of customer preferences at each store.

These initiatives quickly got results, and 2000 saw record sales and earnings. According to the company's Annual Report, "Every day, in more than 226 Stein Mart stores nationwide, our associates greet callers and customers with the phrase, 'It's a great day at Stein Mart; how may I help you?' . . . We are immensely proud to report that through the efforts of our associates, customers, and merchandise partners, Stein Mart enjoyed a full year's worth of 'great days' in 2000." Sales increased to $1.2 billion, with comparable stores sales increasing by 9.7 percent. Net income was $39.4 million, or 91 cents per share.

These results could not be matched in 2001, as the year began with a sluggish economy and slowing sales. In August, Jay, while remaining chairman of the board, relinquished the CEO position to Jack Williams. With Jack elevated to vice chairman, Mike Fisher became president and chief operating officer. The naming of Jack Williams as Stein Mart's chief executive officer represented the first time that the company had been headed by a non-family member. But after more than twenty years together, Jay and Jack had grown so close that their relationship had become more than just a business partnership and Jack had become almost family. Nevertheless, only a month later, the terrorist attacks of September 11 totally redirected Jack's focus and that of other Stein Mart executives.

The horrific events of September 11 severely curtailed shopping. Recognizing that in the aftermath of terrorist attacks people would be more focused on world events than consumer purchases, Jack and his management team directed their efforts at reducing inventory through promotions and markdowns, while negotiating with vendors to limit the amount of incoming goods. With reduced customer activity, store managers placed tight controls on payroll and expenses, and the corporate office instituted a hiring freeze. These quick actions helped to mitigate some of the effects of a slow fourth quarter, that critical time during the retail cycle when most of the sales activity occurs. For the year, sales increased by 9.4 percent, but that can be attributed to the thirty new stores opened that year as well as an additional five weeks of sales results caused by the company's decision to change its fiscal year-end (FYE) to the Saturday closest to January 31, thus making 2001 a thirteen-month year ending February 2, 2002. Comparable store sales declined slightly, and selling and administrative expenses increased dramatically because of the large markdowns, resulting in net income for the year of only $15.4 million, or 37 cents per share.

The results for 2001 had been disappointing, but they could have been much worse without the immediate, proactive steps that management took after September 11.

In February 2002, as Jack prepared to begin his first full year as CEO, he announced that he planned to retire at the end of that year. Then, executive management would unquestionably go outside of the "family." President Mike Fisher would become in February 2003 Stein Mart's new chief executive officer, and Gwen Manto, the company's chief merchandising officer, would be elevated to vice chairman.[4] Throughout 2002, Jack devoted his management efforts to improving Stein Mart's operating performance in what continued to be a lackluster retail environment and facilitating the transition to the new management team.

During his eighteen-month tenure as CEO, Jack worked with Fisher to implement new approaches for streamlining inventory management and to redefine the optimal merchandise mix. In an effort to generate greater sales-per-square-foot productivity, the company began to reallocate floor space in its stores, expanding those areas that had the strongest sales opportunities, such as ladies' clothing and accessories, the Boutique, and gifts, while reducing space for men's and children's clothing. With an increased emphasis on improving the sales performance at existing stores, 2002 saw the opening of only sixteen new stores, the lowest number since 1994. One of the new stores represented a new concept called "collections of Stein Mart." Less than half the size of a typical Stein Mart store, the first "collections of Stein Mart" opened in October in Rolling Hills, California, as a prototype to see if it would allow expansion into resort communities and other targeted markets that might be too small for full-size stores. These initiatives helped Stein Mart to report an improved financial performance for 2002 — net income of $20.7 million, or 50 cents per share. This result did not fully meet management expectations, but as explained in Fisher's first letter to shareholders in the 2002 Annual Report, "Stein Mart's success in 2002 came from making strategic improvements in our core business, and we believe that this progress will prove critical in 2003."

Meanwhile, the management transition process has moved ahead smoothly. Both Jay and Jack express confidence in the new management team. Jack is quick to point out that "I have told Jay and others that he is an entrepreneur and I am a professional executive, and I will be judged, ultimately, on what happens to Stein Mart in the five years after I've gone. If I've done my job properly, we have the people in place and the infrastructure in place that we can take this company from where it is today to where it needs to be five years from now." Jack concludes, "The future is bright for the company, and the business model is sound."

Jay still owns approximately 40 percent of the company and is very much aware that his family name is over the entrance doors of every store. Jay makes it clear that he and Jack both will remain interested directors and be available, when asked, to provide assistance. He anticipates continuing to play the same management role as he has for the last several years. "I'm there to counsel," Jay states. "I certainly have expectations, like any large shareholder would have. I fully feel that those expectations will be met."

And where is the company headed? When asked that question, incoming CEO Mike Fisher responds, "Stein Mart still has and is likely to maintain a very unique niche. We are a hybrid provider of merchandise… [and] we're not like anybody else you can think of." While Fisher envisions increasing store productivity through upgrading technology and developing new marketing and advertising approaches, he doesn't see any need to "reinvent" the company. Stein Mart is, and will remain, a unique combination of several factors: it is an off-price retailer; it is located at off-mall locations that are more convenient for its customers; it processes and presents merchandise differently than its competitors; and it has a strong emphasis on customer service. To Fisher, "Stein Mart in the future is something that looks very similar to what it is today, but is more productive in the way it uses its assets and is able to get to its customers more efficiently."

Even as Stein Mart looks to its future, the company is very aware of its past. And it is fast approaching a significant milestone. January 2005 will mark the one hundredth anniversary of the year Sam Stein, speaking only limited English and having just $43 in his pocket, arrived at Ellis Island. While Sam immigrated to the United States to build a new life for himself, it is doubtful that he could have imagined what would become of the small family business that he started in

Greenville, Mississippi. Such is the power and mystery of dreams. Sam's resourcefulness established the roots of his future success. He began building a dream from personal effort and family values — and his capacity to imagine a greater future for his family and his neighbors. Today the legacy of Sam Stein, and that of his son Jake and grandson Jay, can be seen in the successful chain of retail stores that stretches across the United States in more than 260 locations. Now as a second century of business is about to commence under a new generation of leaders, Stein Mart and its thousands of associates look forward to an exciting future they can only begin to imagine, but one that they all will help to build.

BIBLIOGRAPHICAL ESSAY

Information about Sam Stein and the family that he left behind when emigrating from Russia is sketchy. The best sources of family history are two videotaped interviews with Sam's sister, Tillie Stein Rosenberg, that were conducted by Tillie's daughter and son-in-law, Carolyn and Neil Berman, on October 14 and 15, 1988. Tillie, then in her early eighties, still had vivid memories of her childhood in Russia and her coming to the United States, and she tells some wonderful stories. It is from these interviews that one can identify the family's home as being Amdur, not Bialystok as the Greenville *Daily Democrat-Times* erroneously reported in Sam Stein's obituary. This error undoubtedly resulted from Sam's 1930 trip to Europe to visit his mother, who then lived with one of her daughters in Bialystok, Poland. The Internet website for JewishGen provides a number of valuable links to information about Amdur, especially the first chapter of Sandy Eisen's "Eisen Family and Ancestral Home of Amdur" and "The Grodno Gubernia 1912 Voter List Database." These and other informative websites can be found at <http://www.jewishgen.org>. Amdur, now called Indura, is part of Belarus, and Nicholas P. Vakar's *Belorussia: The Making of a Nation* (Cambridge, Mass., 1956) provides useful background about this region of eastern Europe that at various times has been part of Poland, the Duchy of Lithuania, the Russian Empire, the USSR, and now Belarus.

There are no Stein family memoirs or diaries or letters, but Jake Stein did share his memories of his father (as well as recollections from his own life and business career) in a speech to the Washington County Historical Society on March 24, 1983. Attorney Jerome C. Hafter had a transcript made from the cassette recording of the speech and sent a copy to Jay Stein. In this speech, Jake admits that his memory for dates is weak — "As I give dates and approximate years, I might have mixed up a few because we did not keep any family history. . . . Everything that I tell you is to the best of my memory. If I miss a date [by] a year or two, please forgive me." Jake stated that his father left Russia in 1900, and opened his first store in Greenville in 1903. Research into the immigration records available through The Statue of Liberty-Ellis

Island Foundation at <http://www.ellisisland.org>, however, establishes that Sam Stein did not arrive in New York until January 1905. While Jake's speech is filled with valuable information about Sam Stein's early struggles as a peddler and businessman, dates must be adjusted, where possible, to fit within the historical context of events being described.

Conversations with Stanley Sherman, one of Sam's grandsons, proved helpful in learning about the early years of the Stein family, as Stanley had many opportunities to listen to stories from his grandmother, Fannie Aarenzon Stein, who lived with the Shermans for nearly forty years after being widowed. Also, the William Alexander Percy Memorial Library in Greenville has transcripts from a number of interviews conducted in the late 1970s as part of the Washington County Library System Oral History Project. One of these interviews is with Miss Ollie Bell, who worked as a domestic servant for Sam and Fannie Stein, and later Julius and Sadie Sherman.

Oscar Handlin's *The Uprooted* (Boston, 1951) has long been the standard work on the immigrant experience. Gerald Sorin's *A Time For Building: The Third Migration, 1880-1920* (Baltimore, 1992) is an in-depth study of the massive Jewish exodus from eastern Europe to the U.S. in the late nineteenth and early twentieth century. Sorin provides an excellent summary of living conditions for Jews in Russia's Pale of Settlement and discusses the ocean passage and the conditions upon reaching Ellis Island.

While the number of Jewish immigrants who settled in the South was relatively small, the literature about Southern Jews is expanding. Some seminal essays were collected by editors Leonard Dinnerstein and Mary Dale Palsson in *Jews in the South* (Baton Rouge, La., 1973). Another useful collection was edited by Nathan M. Kaganoff and Melvin I. Urofsky, *"Turn to the South": Essays on Southern Jewry* (Charlottesville, Va., 1979). Most of the Jews in the South, back to colonial days, pursued business interests, as discussed by Steven J. Whitfield in "Commercial Passions: The Southern Jew as Businessman," *American Jewish History*, 71 (March 1982). Two third-generation Jews who chose not to continue in the family retail business, but instead became writers, have contributed very personal and insightful books about growing up Jewish in the South — Eli N. Evans's *The Provincials: A Personal History of Jews in the South* (New York, 1973) and Edward Cohen's *The Peddler's*

Grandson: Growing Up Jewish in Mississippi (Jackson, Miss., 1999). It should be noted that Cohen's experiences growing up in Jackson, where he felt being Jewish made him an "outsider," were far different from Evans's experiences in Durham, North Carolina, where his father had been elected mayor six times, or the Stein family's experiences in Greenville. Nevertheless, Cohen's memoir about the contradictions and compromises involved with trying to be simultaneously both Jewish and Southern should be read. Also useful is Eli Evans's collection of essays, *The Lonely Days Were Sundays: Reflections of a Jewish Southerner* (Jackson, Miss., 1993).

For the early settlement of Jews in Greenville, see Rabbi Leo E. Turitz and Evelyn Turitz's *Jews in Early Mississippi* (Jackson, Miss., 1983) and H. W. Solomon's *The Early History of the Hebrew Union Congregation of Greenville, Mississippi*, second edition (June, 2001), a booklet printed by the synagogue. The issue of religious tolerance in Greenville was discussed by David L. Cohn in his essay, "I've Kept My Name," published in *The Atlantic* in April 1948. Much more recently, memories and attitudes are preserved in the one-hour documentary film *Delta Jews*, written, directed, and produced by Mike DeWitt for Mississippi Educational Television in 1999. This video not only traces the history of Jewish contributions to the Mississippi Delta, but also focuses on the tensions caused by the civil rights problems of the 1950s and 1960s. It discusses the decline in the Jewish population in the Delta after the 1960s and the closing of synagogues throughout the region. Jay Stein is among those interviewed for this video. Also of interest because it includes information about the Grundfest family is Carolyn Gray LeMaster's book *A Corner of the Tapestry: A History of the Jewish Experience in Arkansas, 1820s-1990s* (Fayetteville, Ark., 1994).

There is no solid historical study of Greenville. The one local history, Bern Keating's *A History of Washington County, Mississippi* (Greenville, 1976) written for the Greenville Junior Auxiliary, is a pedestrian effort. Fortunately, however, Greenville has a well-deserved reputation for having produced numerous writers, one of the most prominent being William Alexander Percy. First published in 1941, Percy's autobiographical *Lanterns on the Levee: Recollections of a Planter's Son* (Baton Rouge, La., 1988) is an eloquent reflection on the old Southern way of life that he realized was quickly disappearing. More valuable for this study have been the writings of David L. Cohn. A Greenville native, Cohn returned to Mississippi after an absence of two decades and in 1935 published a personal memoir about the Delta entitled *God Shakes Creation*. After World War II, he added a second part to reflect the changes that had taken place in the Delta during the war and its immediate aftermath and published both parts under the title *Where I Was Born and Raised* (Notre Dame, Ind., 1967). After Cohn's death, an unpublished memoir was found among his papers at the University of Mississippi and, edited by James C. Cobb, was published posthumously as *The Mississippi Delta and the World: The Memoirs of David L. Cohn* (Baton Rouge, La., 1995). For an understanding of the Mississippi Delta, James C. Cobb's *The Most Southern Place on Earth: The Mississippi Delta and the Roots of Regional Identity* (New York, 1992) is a must. Also useful is Tony Dunbar's *Delta Time: A Journey Through Mississippi* (New York, 1990). A critical event in the history of Greenville, and the entire Delta, is the 1927 flood, comprehensively discussed by John M. Barry in *Rising Tide: The Great Mississippi Flood of 1927 and How It Changed America* (New York, 1997). For placing events within a larger state and regional historical context, two helpful volumes were a collection of historical essays edited by Richard Aubrey McLemore, *A History of Mississippi*, Vol. II (Hattiesburg, Miss., 1973), and George Brown Tindall's *The Emergence of the New South*, 1913-1945 (Baton Rouge, La., 1967).

The issue of antisemitism, whether it lies dormant beneath the surface or manifests itself in violent and threatening ways, is a frequent undercurrent in the literature about the Jewish experience. Antisemitism in the South and elsewhere in the U.S. is examined in two books by Leonard Dinnerstein — *Antisemitism in America* (New York, 1994) and a collection of essays, *Uneasy at Home: Antisemitism and the American Jewish Experience* (New York, 1987). The period of greatest tension for Southern Jews occurred during the 1950s and 1960s after the Supreme Court ruled that segregated public schools were unconstitutional and attempts to prevent change plagued Mississippi and other Southern states as resistance to black civil rights intensified. There is a voluminous literature about the South and the civil rights movement. Those works most helpful in this study include: Hodding Carter III, *The South Strikes Back* (Westport, Conn., 1959); James W. Silver, *Mississippi: The Closed Society*, third edition (New York, 1966);

Neil R. McMillen, *The Citizens' Council: Organized Resistance to the Second Reconstruction, 1954-64* (Urbana, Ill. 1971); Mary Aickin Rothschild, *A Case of Black and White: Northern Volunteers and the Southern Freedom Summers, 1964-1965* (Westport, Conn., 1982); Elizabeth Jacoway and David R. Colburn, eds., *Southern Businessmen and Desegregation* (Baton Rouge, La., 1982); Doug McAdam, *Freedom Summer* (New York, 1988); John Dittmer, *Local People: The Struggle for Civil Rights in Mississippi* (Urbana, Ill., 1994); and Clive Webb, *Fight Against Fear: Southern Jews and Black Civil Rights* (Athens, Ga., 2001). Also valuable are Leonard Dinnerstein's essay on "Southern Jewry and the Desegregation Crisis, 1954-1970," published in *American Jewish Historical Quarterly*, 62 (1973), and Seth Forman's "The Unbearable Whiteness of Being Jewish: Desegregation in the South and the Crisis of Jewish Liberalism" in *American Jewish History*, 85 (1997). Any discussion of Mississippi during the civil rights struggles must include the influential editor of Greenville's *Delta Democrat-Times*, who is the subject of Ann Waldron's biography, *Hodding Carter: The Reconstruction of a Racist* (Chapel Hill, N.C., 1993).

Information concerning the woes of the retailing industry during the 1980s and early 1990s, together with details of the flurry of mergers and acquisitions, can be found in news articles in *Fortune, Forbes,* and *Business Week.* The most spectacular of mergers — and the most audacious and unsuccessful — involved Robert Campeau's leveraged buyouts of Allied Stores and Federated Department Stores, which is detailed in John Rothchild's *Going For Broke* (New York, 1991).

Stein Mart received little mention in the business press prior to its IPO. Shortly afterwards, several corporate profiles appeared, including Richard J. Coletti's "Designer Discounter," in *Florida Trend* (September 1992) and Lisa Backman's "The Stein Mart Phenomenon" in the Business & Finance section of the *Tampa Tribune* (December 6, 1993). The Boutique Ladies were highlighted in a front-page *Wall Street Journal* article (December 2, 1992) by Teri Agins, "Clerking at Stein Mart Is a Society Lady's Dream Come True." A more lighthearted look at the Boutique Ladies can be found in Maryln Schwartz's *New Times in the Old South, or Why Scarlett's in Therapy and Tara's Going Condo* (New York, 1993).

There are no company financial records available prior to 1975. The company's Controller's Office made available financial statements, prepared first by a Greenville CPA firm and later by Price Waterhouse, for the years 1975 through 1991. Once Stein Mart became a public company in 1992, its Annual Reports provide valuable information on financial performance and company goals. Copies of management presentations at investment conferences and copies of investment analysts' research reports about the company have been maintained by Stein Mart's Stockholder Relations Department and proved most helpful.

One of the most valuable sources of information about the Stein family and Stein Mart came from personal interviews. Jay Stein agreed to multiple interviews and also facilitated interviews with family members and company employees. Family members interviewed for this project included Jay Stein, Freda Stein, Stanley Sherman, Robert Stein, Carolyn and Neil Berman (by telephone), and Joe Stein Jr. (by telephone). Stein Mart associates interviewed included Jack Williams, Michael D. Fisher, D. Mason Allen, Carl Davis, D. Hunt Hawkins, Gwen K. Manto, Michael D. Ray, Clayton Roberson, Larry Shelton, the first four Boutique Ladies (Jane Carruthers, Jan Bell, Margaret Krausnick, and Ann Stevens), and a number of long-time employees of Greenville Store No. 1 (Adele Billings, James Davis, Rose Whittington Ellis, Mamie Holmes, L. A. Owens, David Shamoon, Sue Thornton, Patsy Welch, and Sue Wright). Also interviewed by telephone were Hodding Carter III, Phil Dobuler, and Frank Hunger.

The Greenville newspapers, the *Daily Democrat-Times* and, after 1938, the *Delta Democrat-Times*, are especially valuable resources, but the lack of detailed indices necessitates considerable amounts of time devoted to searching microfilm copies for revelant articles. After Stein Mart relocated its corporate headquarers to Jacksonville, the *Florida Times-Union* provided on-going news coverage of the company.

NOTES

The notes below cite secondary sources referenced in the text. Quotes and personal recollections from the extensive interviews conducted for this study, as well as from Jake Stein's 1983 speech to the Washington County Historical Society and his sister Tillie Stein Rosenberg's 1988 videotaped interviews, are not cited, as the speaker is generally identified in the narrative. Citations are not included for quotes from the Greenville daily newspapers, Stein Mart Annual Reports, and other sources that also are identified in the text. Financial information for the company from 1975 through 1991 is from financial statements prepared by outside accounting firms, and since 1992 from the company's Annual Reports. The principal source materials used for this study are discussed in the Bibliographical Essay.

Chapter 1

1. Gerald Sorin, *A Time For Building, 1880-1920* (Baltimore, 1992), 12-13, 21-23, 33-34.

2. See H. W. Solomon, "The Early History of the Hebrew Union Congregation of Greenville, Mississippi," 2nd edition (June 2001).

3. Thomas D. Clark, "The Post-Civil War Economy in the South," in Leonard Dinnerstein and Mary Dale Palsson (eds.), *Jews in the South* (Baton Rouge, La., 1973), 163.

4. James C. Cobb (ed.), *The Mississippi Delta and the World: The Memoirs of David L. Cohn* (Baton Rouge, La., 1995), 89-91.

5. *Ibid.*, 89.

6. David L. Cohn, *Where I Was Born and Raised* (Notre Dame, Ind., 1967), 41.

7. George Brown Tindall, *The Emergence of the New South, 1913-1945* (Baton Rouge, La., 1967), 111.

8. William Alexander Percy, *Lanterns on the Levee: Reflections of a Planter's Son* (Baton Rouge, La., 1988), 249.

9. John M. Barry, *Rising Tide: The Great Mississippi Flood of 1927 and How It Changed America* (New York, 1997), 330.

10. *Ibid.*, 328.

Chapter 2

1. Tindall, *Emergence of New South*, 354; William Lincoln Giles, "Agricultural Revolution, 1890-1970," in Richard Aubrey McLemore (ed.), *A History of Mississippi* (Hattiesburg, Miss., 1973), II, 197. According to Giles, "Although historians are inclined to relate the Great Depression to the 1930s, Mississippi farm families lived in a severe economic depression for two decades beginning in 1920. Historical statistics fail to reflect the desperate economic situation of individual, small cotton farmers during that period."

2. John Ray Skates, Jr., "World War II and Its Effects, 1940-1948," in McLemore (ed.), *History of Mississippi*, II, 125.

3. Cohn, *Where I Was Born and Raised*, 229.

4. *Ibid.*, xiv-xv.

5. Harding quoted in a front-page article in the *Delta Democrat-Times* (March 1, 1989) announcing Jake Stein's death.

6. Leonard Dinnerstein, *Antisemitism in America* (New York, 1994), 181.

7. Steven J. Whitfield, "Jews and Other Southerners: Counterpoint and Paradox," in Nathan M. Kagonoff and Melvin I. Urofsky (eds.), *"Turn to the South:" Essays on Southern Jewry* (Charlottesville, Va., 1979), 84.

8. Eli N. Evans, *The Provincials: A Personal History of Jews in the South* (New York, 1973), 212-13.

9. According to Percy, "I came to learn with astonishment that of all the things hated in the South, more hated than the Jew or the Negro or sin itself, is Rome." *Lanterns on the Levee*, 234. Also see, Evans, *The Provincials*, 221-23 and Whitfield, "Jews and Other Southerners," 86-87.

10. David L. Cohn, "I've Kept My Name," *The Atlantic* (April 1948), 44.

11. Leonard Dinnerstein, *Uneasy at Home: Antisemitism and the American Jewish Experience* (New York, 1987), 8-9.

12. Evans, *The Provincials*, 319-20.

13. Hodding Carter III, *The South Strikes Back* (Westport, Conn., 1959), 169-73.

14. Ann Waldron, *Hodding Carter: The Reconstruction of a Racist* (Chapel Hill, N.C.), 254.

15. *Ibid.*, xiii.

16. John Dittmer, *Local People: The Struggle for Civil Rights in Mississippi* (Urbana, Ill., 1994), 67.

17. James W. Silver, *Mississippi: The Closed Society*, (3rd ed.; New York, 1966), 151.

18. Dittmer, *Local People*, 251.

19. Doug McAdam, *Freedom Summer* (New York, 1988), 96, 257-82.

Chapter 3

1. Evans, *The Provincials*, vii.

2. *Ibid.*, 31, 34.

3. *Wall Street Journal*, December 2, 1992. Also see the featured article "Boutique Ladies' Silver Anniversary" in the *Memphis Commercial-Appeal*, September 19, 2002. Written shortly after the twenty-fifth anniversary celebration of the opening of the Memphis store, the article contains many reminiscences about the early days of the first Boutique Ladies.

Chapter 4

1. Quoted in profile of Jack Williams entitled "Stein Mart President Right at Home in Family Business," *Florida Times-Union*, January 29, 1990. It should be pointed out that this close relationship between Jay Stein and Jack Williams caused the author to refer to Williams throughout the text by his first name, Jack, the only person not a member of the Stein family to be so identified. It may be a subtle distinction, but an important one.

2. There is a paucity of written records available for Stein Mart prior to its 1992 IPO. This 1981 document, titled simply "Stein Mart Financial Presentation," was saved by Jack Williams, who provided a copy to the author.

3. *Florida Times-Union*, November 13, 1984.

4. These observations by Jay Stein and Jack Williams are from a corporate profile of Stein Mart, based on interviews with Jay, Jack, and Mason Allen, printed in "The Sun" a quarterly publication of the Jacksonville office of Arthur Andersen (Winter 1991).

Chapter 5

1. Matthew Heller, "Retailing," *Forbes* (January, 13, 1986), 200.

2. David Pauly, "Retailing's Hard Times," *Newsweek* (August 8, 1988), 46.

3. The retailing woes of the late 1980s and early 1990s are detailed in numerous news articles. See Susan Caminiti, "What Ails Retailing," *Fortune* (January 30, 1989), 61, 64; Bill Saporito, "Retailing's Winners & Losers," *Fortune* (December 18, 1989), 69-78; "Retailing: Who Will Survive?" *Business Week* (November 26, 1990), 134-37, 140, 144; "Fewer Rings on the Cash Registers," *Business Week* (January 14, 1991), 85; and Rita Koselka, "Fading Into History," *Forbes* (August 19, 1991), 70-71.

4. In mid-November 2003, while the manuscript for this corporate history was being prepared for publication, Gwen Manto resigned as vice chairman and a member of the company's board of directors. The article in the business section of the *Florida Times-Union* (November 11, 2003) stated that Manto "resigned to pursue other interests" and that Stein Mart would immediately begin a search for a new chief merchandising officer.

ACKNOWLEDGMENTS

This history of Stein Mart would not have been possible without the support and cooperation of Jay Stein. When first approached about this project, Jay seemed hesitant, but he soon warmed to the idea. Jay gave generously of his time and agreed to a series of taped interviews that provided valuable information and insights into the Stein family and their business ventures. He also made introductions to other family members and encouraged them to visit with me.

Part of the enjoyment of this project has been the opportunity to meet members of the Stein family. Jay's mother, Freda, is a charming and gracious woman. She showed great hospitality during my research visits to Greenville, inviting me to her home and ensuring that we ate at the city's best restaurants, including a memorable visit to the famous Doe's Eat Place. As this project neared completion in early 2003, Miss Freda finally stopped working at the store, moving from Greenville to Jacksonville to be closer to her son.

I enjoyed numerous discussions, both in Greenville and by phone, with Stanley Sherman, who shared his wealth of knowledge about the family, as well as his insights into local and state history. In addition, Stanley helped to gather photographs for this book from his personal collection of family photos. Robert Stein and Joe Stein Jr. also shared family memories and photographs, as did Carolyn and Neil Berman. I especially want to thank Neil for helping to clarify family history questions during a number of phone conversations and for suggesting some subtle changes after a careful reading of an early draft.

The executives and employees of Stein Mart were helpful, cooperative, and enthusiastic about this project. Jack Williams always made time to answer my questions and explain important details about the company's strategic focus and operational dynamics. He provided insightful comments about the business acumen of his close friend and business associate, Jay Stein. Jack has a tremendous memory, and I am grateful for his careful reading of an early draft of the manuscript and his gentle manner in pointing out areas where I had become confused or made factual errors. Mike Fisher suggested several critical revisions that saved me from considerable embarrassment. It needs to be emphasized, however, that while Jay, Jack, and Mike all critiqued the manuscript, none of them placed any restrictions on my research efforts and none sought to alter my interpretations. I greatly appreciate their confidence in allowing me the independence necessary to research and write the company history, and I acknowledge that any errors of fact or interpretation are mine alone.

I want to thank all of the Stein Mart associates, past and present, who agreed to be interviewed for this project. A complete listing of their names is included in the bibliography. Carl Davis, Larry Shelton, and Clayton Roberson not only agreed to lengthy interviews, but assisted with numerous follow-up questions. Clayton also allowed me access to copies of financial reports and related CPA studies from the period prior to the 1992 IPO. Susan Edelman, Director of Stockholder Relations, provided a complete set of Annual Reports for the years since Stein Mart became a public company in 1992, as well as copies of company presentations at investment conferences and research reports from various Wall Street analysts. David Mohamed, manager of Store No. 1 in Greenville, coordinated my meeting schedule with current and retired employees from the company's flagship store, graciously giving up his office one day so that I could conduct these interviews. Jane Carruthers hosted a delightful luncheon at the Memphis Country Club with "the original four Boutique Ladies." It was an afternoon filled with much laughter and wonderful stories about the Boutique (as I frantically struggled to take notes), and afterwards Jane gave me photos, letters, employee newsletters, and other memorabilia that she had saved over the past twenty-five years.

Anyone interested in Greenville's rich history should start with a visit to Benji Nelkin. Not only is his real estate office filled with an eclectic collection of photos, newspaper articles, and other artifacts, but Benji is also the curator of the historical exhibits at the Hebrew Union Temple. I appreciate Benji giving me a personal tour of the synagogue and sharing his extensive knowledge of local history, as well as allowing use of several of his photographs of downtown Greenville. I also enjoyed the hospitality of Greenville Mayor Paul Artman, who not only gave me a first-hand glimpse of how to respond to constituent problems, but also allowed access to the city council records.

I want to thank the research librarians at the William Alexander Percy Library in Greenville for their assistance during my research trips, and the Inter-Library Loan staff at the Thomas G. Carpenter Library at the University of North Florida for their help in obtaining copies of journal articles and microfilm of the Greenville newspapers.

A special thanks goes to Hugh Jones, a fiend and former colleague at Barnett Bank. Hugh, then president of the Barnett Bank of Jacksonville, obtained Stein Mart's banking business when the company relocated to Jacksonville and also persuaded Jay Stein to serve on Barnett's Board of Directors. It was Hugh who first suggested to his friend Jay that he meet with me to discuss a possible Stein Mart history. Thanks to two other former Barnett executives — Roland Kennedy and Albert Ernest — who also recommended me to Jay.

Photographs and visual materials, especially including the selections reproduced in this book, have added to my understanding and appreciation of the people and the history of Stein Mart. I gratefully acknowledge the William Alexander Percy Library in Greenville, Mississippi, for permission to reproduce photo 6 (page 17) and the *Florida Times-Union* (Jacksonville, Florida) for permission to reproduce photos 42 (page 111) and 45 (page 115).

Most of the photographs in this book — other than those from Stein Mart, Inc., and its corporate publications — were contributed by members of the Stein family from their personal collections: Jay Stein (1, 8, 15, 23, 24, 25, 26, 34, 43, 44, and 48); Stanley Sherman (3, 4, 12, 13, 14, 16, 18, and 19); Joe Stein Jr. (10); and Neil and Carolyn Berman (2 and 5). Other photographs were provided by Benji Nelkin (7, 17, 20, and 21), Jane Carruthers (27 and 28), and Larry Shelton (32 and 53). Copies of advertisements came from scrapbooks housed in Stein Mart's Marketing Department.

I want to thank Numgi Lee Abdel for typing several drafts of the manuscript, no easy task given the deficiencies in my handwriting. I also wish to express my appreciation to the University of Tampa Press for publishing this corporate history. I have worked with Richard Mathews, the director of the press, on a previous book, and again Richard has proved to be an excellent editor. I value his insights and his suggestions that always improve my writing efforts, and over the past few years I have come to regard him as not only an editor, but a friend. Richard's assistant, Sean Donnelly, has once more done an excellent job in helping to coordinate the myriad tasks necessary to bring this project to completion.

Finally, I need to express thanks to my wife Carole, who, as always, has supported my research and writing endeavors. I do not enjoy shopping, and often have gone to great lengths to avoid accompanying Carole and our daughters on trips to the shopping malls. So when I first told Carole — a loyal Stein Mart customer — that I had a meeting scheduled with Jay Stein, she asked if I had ever been in a Stein Mart store. Like most wives, she already knew the answer to her question. She took me to the closest Stein Mart, and told me all about what she liked best — from the bargain prices to the Boutique. A year later, I must confess that I too now shop at Stein Mart, and have my own "Preferred Customer" card.

David J. Ginzl
May 2003

INDEX

This is a selected index of names and subjects in the book. Page numbers in bold italics indicate references to photographs or illustrations.

About the Author

David J. Ginzl earned a B.A. in history from Hartwick College and completed an MA and Ph.D. in American history from Syracuse University. He joined Barnett Bank in 1977 and during his twenty-year career held various senior management positions in loan administration and credit policy, the last being Director of Business Risk Management and Credit Policy for Barnett Banks, Inc. After the sale of Barnett to NationsBank in 1998, Ginzl became president of the nonprofit Barnett Historic Preservation Foundation, Inc., gathering historical records relating to the bank's history and writing two books, *Images of America: Barnett Bank* (Arcadia Publishing, 2000) and *Barnett: The Story of "Florida's Bank"* (University of Tampa Press, 2001). The reviewer in the *Florida Historical Quarterly* said that *Barnett: The Story of "Florida's Bank"* was "the best book ever written on commercial banking in Florida, and indeed one of the best volumes ever produced on the economic and business history of the entire state. Moreover, it ranks among the best publications on a financial services firm headquartered anywhere in the United States." Ginzl has written numerous articles and book reviews for historical journals and banking magazines. He lives in Jacksonville, Florida, with his wife, Carole, and spends his time writing, teaching, and doing bank consulting.